Communication & Administration of Intercollegiate Athletics

For use in COMM 4507 taught by
Dr. Hayden Coombs at
Southern Utah University.

1st Edition - 2024

ISBN: 9798884792807

Coombs, H. V. (2024). *Communication and administration of intercollegiate athletics* (1st ed.). KDP.

Printed by Kindle Direct Publishing in the United States of America.

First printed edition 2024.

www.haydencoombs.com

For Kyle Newhouse.

I wouldn't be here without you, buddy. The next round of KFC and NBA Jam is on me.

Proceeds from the sale of this textbook go to a scholarship fund for sports communication students at Southern Utah University.

Contents

Chapter 1
Why Do Sports Matter?

"Sport has the power to change the world. It has the power to inspire, it has the power to unite people in a way that little else does. It speaks to youth in a language they understand. Sport can create hope, where once there was only despair. It is more powerful than governments in breaking down racial barriers. It laughs in the face of all types of discrimination."
- Nelson Mandela, 2000

Upon successful completion of this unit, students will be able to:

- Recognize how sports serve as a unifying force across diverse societies, fostering a sense of community and belonging.
- Acknowledge the comprehensive health benefits of sports, including physical fitness, mental well-being, and the promotion of healthy lifestyles.
- Articulate how sports contribute to the development of essential life skills such as discipline, teamwork, leadership, and resilience.
- Understand the role of sports in expressing and preserving cultural identity and facilitating cultural exchange and understanding.
- Evaluate the significant economic contributions of the sports industry to local, national, and global economies.
- Examine how sports serve as platforms for education, social change, and the promotion of equality and social justice.

Why do sports matter?

Why does the university let me teach a series of courses on sports administration, communication, and management?

What's the point of all of this?

Sports have long been an integral part of human society, serving as a microcosm of life's challenges, achievements, and the resilience of humankind. They offer more than just physical benefits; they provide a platform for social interaction, cultural expression, and the cultivation of values that resonate deeply within communities and individuals alike. This chapter delves into the multifaceted reasons why sports matter to our society and underscores their importance in fostering unity, personal development, and cultural identity.

The Social Fabric and Unity

Sports, in their essence, are much more than mere games or physical contests; they are a conduit for unity, capable of bridging gaps that often seem insurmountable in other areas of life. This unique ability of sports to bring people together extends across social, economic, and cultural boundaries, creating a fabric of unity woven from the diverse threads of society. At the heart of major sporting events like the Olympics or the FIFA World Cup lies an unparalleled global celebration, where millions of people, regardless of nationality, race, or religion, unite in their passion for the game. These events do more than entertain; they foster a sense of global community and understanding, shining a light on the unifying power of sports. This shared experience of jubilation in victory and commiseration in defeat transcends spoken language, becoming a universal dialogue of humanity.

Furthermore, the impact of sports on unity and community engagement is equally profound at a local level. From neighborhood basketball courts to school sports days, and from local football leagues to community marathons, sports serve as vital communal hubs. They offer common ground for individuals from various backgrounds, ideologies, and lifestyles, encouraging them to come together with a shared purpose. Through supporting local teams, volunteering at sports events, or simply playing together in public spaces, people forge bonds of friendship, respect, and understanding. These activities strengthen the social fabric of communities, fostering a sense of belonging, collective identity, and pride within neighborhoods and regions.

Sports also act as a powerful tool for social inclusion, providing platforms for marginalized or underserved communities to be seen, heard, and celebrated. Through inclusive sports programs and initiatives, individuals who might otherwise feel isolated—due to disability, socioeconomic status, or cultural differences—find opportunities for participation and recognition. This inclusivity not only enriches the lives of those directly involved but also educates and sensitizes the broader community to the value of diversity and the strength it brings.

Moreover, the role of sports in uniting people can have a cascading effect on societal health and well-being. By fostering an environment of teamwork and mutual support, sports can contribute to reducing instances of social isolation and loneliness, while promoting a culture of active, engaged citizenship. The sense of unity and community belonging that sports engender is instrumental in creating safer, cohesive societies where individuals feel connected to and responsible for one another.

Sports embody a universal language of camaraderie, resilience, and shared humanity, making them a fundamental pillar in the architecture of social unity and community spirit. Their ability to assemble diverse groups of individuals around common goals and joys is a testament to their enduring power to strengthen the social fabric and cultivate a sense of belonging and pride among communities across the globe.

Health and Well-being

The health benefits of regular sports participation are well-documented, ranging from improved physical health, such as better cardiovascular function and weight management, to mental health benefits, including reduced symptoms of depression and anxiety. Sports instill the importance of physical activity in maintaining a healthy lifestyle, encouraging habits that can last a lifetime. Furthermore, participation in sports from a young age teaches children the value of regular exercise, setting the foundation for a healthy adulthood.

Personal Development and Life Skills

The role of sports in personal development extends far beyond the boundaries of physical fitness, venturing into the realm of life skills cultivation that participants can apply in various aspects of their lives. Engagement in sports activities instills a deep sense of commitment, discipline, and the essence of hard work, which are not only crucial for achieving success in the competitive sports arena but are equally vital in navigating the complexities of everyday life. Through consistent training, athletes are taught the importance of setting realistic goals and the dedication required to diligently pursue these objectives, thereby fostering a proactive approach to personal and professional challenges.

Moreover, the dynamic and often unpredictable nature of sports provides a fertile ground for developing a robust sense of resilience and perseverance among participants. This environment encourages athletes to confront obstacles head-on, equipping them with the strength to withstand failures and the agility to rebound from setbacks with enhanced determination. The lessons learned in overcoming these challenges are invaluable, offering insights into the significance of maintaining a positive outlook and the resilience required to adapt and thrive in the face of adversity.

Team sports, in particular, serve as an excellent microcosm for the broader societal and professional landscapes, emphasizing the critical importance of teamwork, effective communication, and leadership. Within the structure of a team, individuals learn to collaborate towards a common goal, valuing the unique contributions of each member while fostering an environment of mutual respect and support. This collaborative spirit is coupled with the development of strong communication skills, as athletes learn to articulate their ideas clearly, listen attentively to their teammates, and provide constructive feedback, thereby enhancing the overall cohesion and efficiency of the team.

Leadership skills are also honed in the sporting context, as athletes are often called upon to lead by example, motivate their peers, and make strategic decisions under pressure. These experiences provide valuable lessons in leadership that are applicable in various settings beyond sports, from the workplace to community involvement. Through sports, individuals gain insights into the qualities of effective leaders, including the ability to inspire and unite others, the foresight to plan strategically, and the humility to learn from both successes and failures.

Sports offer a comprehensive platform for personal growth, teaching participants a wide array of life skills that are highly prized in both personal and professional spheres. From fostering a disciplined approach to goal setting and execution to cultivating resilience, teamwork, communication, and leadership, the contributions of sports to personal development are profound and far-reaching, underscoring the integral role of sports in shaping well-rounded, capable individuals ready to make meaningful contributions to society.

Sportsmanship

Sportsmanship stands at the heart of athletics, embodying values that elevate the spirit of competition beyond mere victory and defeat. It's a concept that transcends the boundaries of fields, courts, and arenas, speaking to the very essence of human dignity, respect, and integrity. Sportsmanship is not just about adhering to the rules of the game but about fostering a culture of respect, fairness, and empathy among competitors. It is about shaking hands with your opponent before and after the match, acknowledging their skills, and appreciating the shared effort to excel and push each other towards greatness. This ethos enriches the sporting experience, making it more than a test of physical prowess—it becomes a celebration of shared humanity, teaching lessons that resonate far beyond the final whistle.

Furthermore, the importance of sportsmanship is highlighted in its capacity to teach valuable life lessons to athletes and spectators alike. Through sportsmanship, individuals learn about the grace of accepting defeat and the humility of victory, the importance of mutual respect, and the strength found in teamwork and collaboration. These lessons are vital, as they transcend the realm of sports, guiding individuals in personal and professional challenges. In fostering sportsmanship, sports not only contribute to the personal development of individuals but also to the cultivation of a society that values fairness, respect, and dignity. This profound impact underscores the vital role sportsmanship plays in the world of athletics and its significance in shaping character and community ethos.

Unwritten rules in sports are traditions that embody the spirit of sportsmanship, signifying respect and honor among competitors beyond the explicit regulations. These tacit norms—whether it's not celebrating too exuberantly after a score to avoid demeaning the opponent, or the act of kicking the ball out of play when a player is injured—serve as the moral compass guiding athletes' conduct. They reflect an understanding that, while the drive to win is fierce, maintaining dignity and mutual respect holds a higher value. Adherence to these unwritten rules fosters a culture of integrity and fairness, reinforcing the idea that how one plays the game is as important as the outcome. In essence, these traditions underscore the profound connection between sportsmanship and the unspoken agreements that honor the game's spirit, ensuring it remains a noble pursuit of excellence, camaraderie, and respect.

Cultural Expression and Identity

Sports are not just physical endeavors but are deeply imbued with the cultures and histories from which they emerge. They serve as a vibrant tapestry, weaving together the threads of societal norms, values, and collective memory, thus playing an indispensable role in both the expression and preservation of cultural identity. Traditional sports and games, in particular, act as living repositories of a community's heritage, encapsulating centuries of history, folklore, and societal values. These activities do more than entertain; they are a conduit through which a society's way of life, its struggles, triumphs, and underlying ethos, are celebrated and revered.

The participation in, and support of, traditional sports enables individuals to engage directly with their cultural heritage, fostering a sense of belonging and identity. This engagement is not passive; it is an active affirmation of one's roots and an acknowledgment of the rich tapestry of practices and rituals passed down through generations. Furthermore, traditional sports often play a pivotal role in cultural ceremonies and celebrations, serving as a focal point around which communities gather to mark significant occasions, celebrate communal achievements, and reinforce social bonds.

Moreover, the international and cross-cultural appeal of sports offers a unique platform for cultural exchange. Through the global language of sports, individuals from diverse backgrounds come into contact, sharing aspects of their cultural identities and heritage. This exchange is not a one-way street but a dynamic interaction that can lead to a deeper appreciation of diversity, fostering mutual respect and understanding among disparate groups. Through sports, barriers are broken down, and common ground is found, not in the erasure of differences, but in the celebration of them.

Sports are a mirror reflecting the multifaceted nature of human societies. They are a means by which cultural identities are not only expressed and preserved but also shared and enriched. Through participation in sports, individuals contribute to the preservation of their culture while also laying the groundwork for its transmission to future generations. In this way, sports ensure that the flame of cultural identity continues to burn brightly, illuminating the path from the past, through the present, and into the future.

Economic Impact

The economic significance of sports cannot be understated. The sports industry generates millions of jobs worldwide and contributes significantly to national and local economies. From the construction of stadiums to the hosting of major sporting events, sports stimulate economic development and can revitalize communities. Additionally, the sports sector fosters entrepreneurship and innovation, from advancements in sports equipment and technology to the burgeoning field of sports analytics.

Education and Social Change

Sports have the power to educate and bring about social change. Through sports, individuals learn about fairness, justice, and equality, with the playing field often serving as a space where social issues are highlighted and addressed. Initiatives like Title IX in the United States have used sports as a platform to promote gender equality, providing women and girls equal opportunities to participate in sports. Moreover, sports programs targeted at youth in underserved communities can provide an alternative to negative influences, teaching valuable life lessons and offering a pathway to education and personal growth.

The profundity of sports within society transcends the mere act of physical engagement, emerging as a dynamic force that unites individuals across a mosaic of backgrounds. Sports arenas transform into hallowed grounds where shared passions override differences, cultivating a sense of community and collective identity that ripples out into broader societal constructs. The influence of sports on personal growth is equally formidable; as live classrooms, they impart critical life skills such as discipline, leadership, and strategic thinking. This educational facet underscores the ability of sports to act as a formative influence on character and resilience, where the trials and triumphs on the field become valuable lessons for life's myriad challenges.

Culturally, sports represent a dualistic narrative, serving both as a reflection of traditions and a platform for new expressions of identity. Economically, they are potent engines that drive job creation, innovation, and community revitalization, underpinning significant sectors of global economies. The intrinsic value of sports also extends to their capacity as educational vectors and harbingers of social change. Through sports, barriers are dismantled, social norms are challenged, and the seeds of progress are sown, as seen in movements like Title IX, which leveraged the landscape of athletics to advance gender equality.

The true significance of sports lies in their universal language, one that articulates the values, aspirations, and shared struggles of humanity. They encapsulate the essence of the human experience, echoing the complexity and diversity of society. Through this lens, sports are not just games but a cultural phenomenon that resonates with the intrinsic need for connection, celebration, and growth, securing their place as a cornerstone of society's fabric.

Discussion Questions

- In what ways can sports serve as a platform for cultural exchange and understanding among different communities?
- Discuss instances where sports have successfully bridged social, economic, or cultural divides within a community or on a global scale.
- Can sports always be considered a unifying force, or are there instances where they might exacerbate divisions?
- Reflect on the life skills that participation in sports can teach individuals. How do these skills transfer to other areas of life outside of sports?
- Discuss the concept of resilience as learned through sports. How does overcoming challenges in sports prepare individuals for obstacles in other aspects of life?
- Discuss the potential of sports programs in underserved communities to effect positive change. Can sports be a viable pathway to education and personal growth for youth in these areas?
- Analyze the physical and mental health benefits of regular sports participation. How can communities encourage active lifestyles through sports?
- Consider the role of sports in promoting a holistic approach to health and well-being. How do sports contribute not just to physical fitness, but also to mental and social health?
- What does sportsmanship teach us about ethics and moral behavior both in and out of sports? Discuss the importance of fairness, respect, and integrity in sports.
- How do sports confront and address ethical dilemmas and social issues? Provide examples where sports have been a catalyst for discussing and resolving ethical concerns.

Case Study 1.1: The Unifying Power of Sports

Sports have long been recognized not just as forms of entertainment or physical activity but as powerful platforms for social cohesion, cultural expression, and personal development. They transcend geographical, social, and cultural boundaries, bringing people together in ways few other activities can. This case study explores the multifaceted impact of sports on society, focusing on a specific event that exemplifies the unifying power of sports.

The Event

In 1995, South Africa hosted the Rugby World Cup, a pivotal moment not just in the realm of sports but in the history of the nation itself. Coming shortly after the end of apartheid, a system of institutionalized racial segregation and discrimination, South Africa was a country in need of healing and unity. Nelson Mandela, the country's first black president, recognized the potential of sports to transcend differences and unify the nation.

The Impact

- National Unity: The South African team, known as the Springboks, historically represented the white minority. Mandela's act of donning the Springbok jersey and supporting the team became a powerful symbol of reconciliation and unity. His presence at the final match and the country's victory served as a unifying moment for all South Africans, bridging the country's deep racial divides.
- International Recognition: South Africa's victory on the world stage, coupled with the powerful narrative of reconciliation and unity, brought international acclaim and attention. It showcased the potential of sports to contribute to healing and understanding in post-conflict societies.
- Personal Development: The event highlighted the role of sports in fostering qualities such as leadership, resilience, and teamwork. Players and fans alike were inspired by the values of hard work, dedication, and the pursuit of excellence.
- Cultural Expression: The Rugby World Cup served as a platform for expressing and celebrating South Africa's diverse cultures. It helped to strengthen national identity and pride, showcasing the country's rich cultural heritage to the world.

Discussion

- Analyze Nelson Mandela's leadership in leveraging the Rugby World Cup as an opportunity for national unity. What does this say about the potential of sports to effect social change?
- Discuss the impact of the Springboks' victory on the process of reconciliation in South Africa. Can sports always serve as a bridge in divided societies?
- Reflect on the cultural and social implications of the event. How did it contribute to a sense of national identity and pride among South Africans?
- Consider the long-term effects of the 1995 Rugby World Cup on

South African society and on the international perception of South Africa. How have sports continued to play a role in the country's development?

Case Study 1.2: Empowerment Through Sports

Sports often emerge as more than a test of physical prowess; they are platforms for empowerment, personal development, and societal transformation. This case study will examine the profound impact of sports on a group of individuals within a correctional facility for juvenile offenders, known as the Gainesville Tornadoes, and how a single act of sportsmanship from their opponents provided a transformative experience.

The Event

Gainesville State School, a correctional facility in Texas, had a football team composed of youth offenders, known as the "Tornadoes." The Tornadoes had an unusual predicament; they played all their games on the road and without the support of a cheering crowd. This changed during one particular game when their opponents, led by Coach Kris Hogan, asked half of their own fans to cheer for the Gainesville Tornadoes. This single gesture shifted the atmosphere from adversarial competition to compassionate support, creating an environment where the young men from Gainesville could feel valued and recognized, perhaps for the first time in their lives.

The Impact

- Personal Empowerment: For the Gainesville players, this experience was transformative. Used to being identified by their offenses, they were suddenly just football players, part of a team, and worth cheering for. It offered them a new narrative about their identity and their place in the community.
- Community Response: This event highlighted the power of empathy and community spirit. The decision by Coach Hogan and the fans to support the opposing team spoke volumes about the role of sports in building inclusive communities. It showed that sports could transcend traditional roles of winners and losers, focusing instead on collective human experience.
- Societal Reflection: The widespread positive response to the story of the Gainesville Tornadoes reflects society's recognition of the need for inclusive and rehabilitative approaches within the juvenile justice system. It sparked conversations about the role of empathy in reform and the potential for sports to rehabilitate and empower those who have been marginalized by society.

18

Discussion
- Analyze how the act of sportsmanship experienced by the Gainesville Tornadoes reflects the transformative power of sports in personal development and rehabilitation.
- Consider the leadership role played by Coach Hogan in facilitating this act of sportsmanship. How can sports leaders promote similar values in their communities?
- Discuss how this event goes beyond sportsmanship on the field and touches on broader social values and the rehabilitation of youth offenders.

Chapter 2
What Makes College Sports Unique Business?

Understanding what makes the business of college sports unique requires examining a confluence of factors that differentiate collegiate athletics from both professional sports and other industries. College sports in the United States are steeped in tradition, emotion, and a unique governance structure that weaves together education, entertainment, and business in a way that is inherently distinct from any other sector. This chapter will explore the intricate business components of collegiate athletics, emphasizing their peculiarities and the multifaceted challenges and opportunities they present.

Upon successful completion of this unit, students will be able to:

- Identify the distinctive economic, social, and cultural dynamics that render college sports a unique business within the larger sports industry landscape.
- Analyze the financial frameworks and revenue models prevalent in college athletics, including the implications of fundraising, media rights, and merchandising.
- Examine the regulatory environment of college sports, focusing on governance bodies like the NCAA, and how these institutions shape the business of collegiate athletics.
- Evaluate the balance between commercial interests and educational values in college sports, including the impact on student-athlete welfare and academic integrity.
- Discuss the ethical considerations in the commercialization of college sports, including equity in gender and minority participation, and the debate over student-athlete compensation.
- Explore the career opportunities within college sports business, understanding the required skills and competencies for various roles in athletic administration, compliance, marketing, and support services.

The Emotional Economy of College Sports

The realm of college sports operates within an emotional economy that is deeply entwined with the fabric of educational institutions and their communities. At the heart of this unique business model lies the unwavering dedication of its stakeholders, encompassing not only the students and alumni but also local supporters and academic affiliates. This profound emotional investment transcends the typical consumer-producer relationship seen in other sports sectors, creating an ecosystem where passion and loyalty are as critical as any financial metric.

The binding force of this economy is the powerful sense of identity that stakeholders derive from their association with a college sports team. This allegiance often stems from a personal connection to the alma mater—a shared history, an unwavering pride in institutional achievements, and a collective embrace of educational and athletic excellence. For many, support for their college team is an expression of personal and communal identity, reflecting a legacy of shared experiences and values. It's this emotional resonance that transforms fans into lifelong advocates of their collegiate programs.

In this emotionally charged market, consumer behavior is unique and multifaceted. Fans are not mere spectators; they are an integral part of the collegiate athletics narrative. Their support is demonstrated through a spectrum of engagement: they might don the team colors with fervor, traveling great distances to fill stadiums, or they may celebrate their team's achievements with the fervor of personal triumphs. Alumni and students, in particular, showcase an enduring loyalty that often continues long after graduation, underscoring the role of sports as a cornerstone of their college experience. They contribute not only through financial means, such as purchasing season tickets or contributing to booster clubs, but also through intangible means, including mentoring athletes, offering professional opportunities to graduates, and advocating for the institution's academic programs.

This emotional commitment also manifests in the willingness to donate to athletic programs, which often translates into substantial financial support for facilities, scholarships, and program enhancements. These contributions are made not in expectation of a return on investment but out of a genuine desire to uplift the institution and its athletic endeavors. The cycle of giving back enhances the college's ability to attract new talent, further invest in its programs, and improve its facilities, creating a virtuous circle fueled by emotional allegiance.

Moreover, the sense of community and belonging that college sports engender often leads to the formation of traditions and rituals that become part of the institution's lore. From tailgating before games to singing the school's fight song, these traditions foster a culture that unites past, present, and future generations. Fans and students may volunteer their time, participate in game-day rituals, and engage in philanthropic events, all of which contribute to the vibrant and communal spirit of college athletics.

This emotional economy of college sports, therefore, adds a complex layer to its business model—one that values emotional ties as much as financial gains, shaping a sports culture that is as rich in sentiment as it is in spectacle. It is an economy of heartfelt engagement, where the metrics of success are painted not just in the black and red of financial statements but in the colors of loyalty, tradition, and the enduring spirit of collegiate unity.

BIRGing and CORFing

Basking in Reflected Glory (BIRGing) is a psychological phenomenon where individuals associate themselves with the success of others, such as sports teams, to enhance their own self-esteem and sense of belonging. Fans wearing team jerseys, sharing victories on social media, and participating in victory parades are common examples of BIRGing. This behavior underscores the deep emotional connection fans have with their teams, serving as a source of pride and joy. The commercialization of fandom leverages this connection by marketing sports merchandise, exclusive memberships, and experiences that allow fans to outwardly display their affiliation and celebrate their team's success, thus turning fan loyalty and pride into a profitable venture for sports franchises and related businesses.

Conversely, Cutting Off Reflected Failure (CORFing) involves distancing oneself from a team or athlete following a loss or failure, as a way to protect one's self-esteem. Fans might downplay their allegiance, criticize the team, or completely dissociate from them in the wake of defeat. In terms of commercialization, CORFing presents a challenge to maintaining fan engagement and loyalty. To combat this, marketing strategies often focus on narratives of resilience, comeback stories, and loyalty rewards, encouraging fans to stand by their teams in tough times. This approach not only helps in retaining fan base during losing seasons but also capitalizes on the emotional rollercoaster of sports, turning even failures into opportunities for deepening fan connections and opening avenues for merchandise sales, ticket promotions, and loyalty-driven marketing campaigns.

Financial Landscape

Despite the non-profit status of educational institutions, college sports have become a significant economic force. The financial structure of collegiate athletics often reflects a delicate balance between generating revenue and maintaining the educational integrity of the institution. This balance is crucial because, unlike professional sports teams that primarily exist to generate profits for owners, college sports programs serve broader institutional goals, including enhancing the campus experience, building community relations, and upholding the educational mission of the institution. Yet, the revenue from ticket sales, broadcasting rights, and merchandising for high-profile sports like football and basketball can rival those of professional teams, highlighting the economic potency of college sports as a business.

The unique governance structure of collegiate sports also plays a role in its financial model. The National Collegiate Athletic Association (NCAA), conferences, and individual schools create a multi-layered regulatory environment that governs everything from TV contracts to athlete recruitment. With the recent changes in athlete compensation laws and the conversation around image and likeness rights, the NCAA's traditional stance on amateurism is being challenged, potentially leading to new revenue streams and business models within college sports.

Operational Intricacies

Collegiate athletics departments operate as integrated units within educational institutions, aligning their operations with academic schedules, campus policies, and broader educational goals. This integration mandates that athletic departments balance the commercial aspects of sports management with the educational priorities of the institution. Operational challenges include facility management, where stadiums and arenas must serve both sporting events and other institutional needs; student-athlete welfare, where the health and academic success of the athletes are as critical as their performance on the field; and compliance with NCAA regulations, where failure to adhere can result in sanctions that affect both finances and reputation.

One of the most distinctive features of college sports is the recruitment and development of student-athletes. Unlike professional sports, where talent acquisition is primarily a financial transaction, collegiate programs navigate the recruitment process with an eye towards both athletic potential and academic fit. The concept of 'scholar-athletes' is central to the collegiate sports model, emphasizing the dual commitment to athletics and academics. This adds an extra layer to the business of college sports, as programs must invest in academic support services and ensure compliance with academic performance standards.

Commercialization of College Sports

The commercialization of college sports has transformed the landscape of collegiate athletics, turning it into a multibillion-dollar industry. This metamorphosis is evident in the extensive broadcasting deals, lucrative sponsorships, and marketing agreements that have become synonymous with college sports. Institutions and athletic programs vie for television rights and apparel deals that not only bring significant financial gain but also increase the visibility and prestige of their teams. Such commercial interests have led to the construction of state-of-the-art facilities and the hiring of top-tier coaching staff, all in the pursuit of athletic excellence and, implicitly, greater revenue. This influx of money into college sports has undeniably elevated the quality of play and the athlete's college experience but has also raised questions about the prioritization of revenue over the educational mission of these institutions.

Amidst the financial windfall, the commercialization of college sports has sparked a debate about the role and treatment of student-athletes who are the linchpin of this lucrative enterprise. As television deals and sponsorship agreements swell the coffers of colleges and universities, the athletes often receive a minimal share of the bounty, limited to scholarships that cover tuition, room, and board. This discrepancy has led to a growing chorus of voices advocating for compensation beyond traditional scholarships, arguing that athletes should share in the revenues they help generate. The debate touches on the very foundation of college sports, challenging the amateur status of college athletes and calling for a reevaluation of policies to ensure fair compensation for their contributions, both on and off the field.

This commercialization has had profound implications for the culture and integrity of collegiate athletics. As financial considerations become increasingly paramount, concerns about the erosion of academic values and the overemphasis on athletic success have surfaced. The pressure to win and generate revenue can lead to compromised academic standards for athletes and unethical behavior among programs desperate to maintain a competitive edge. This environment challenges the balance between athletics and academics, prompting a reexamination of the role that commercial interests should play in the realm of higher education. Ultimately, the commercialization of college sports calls for a thoughtful dialogue about maintaining the integrity of the educational mission, ensuring the well-being of student-athletes, and fostering a healthy balance between financial gain and the core values of collegiate athletics.

Market Dynamics and the Role of Media

The symbiosis between college sports and media rights agreements constitutes a cornerstone of the financial model underpinning collegiate athletics. These contracts, which can span years and involve millions of dollars, have become more intricate as the scope of media has expanded. For powerhouse conferences, media rights often comprise the lion's share of revenue, eclipsing even ticket sales and alumni donations. The negotiations for these rights extend beyond the individual institutions and encapsulate entire conferences, exemplifying a collaborative approach to maximize exposure and profitability. This collaborative strategy has led to the advent of conference-specific television networks, further amplifying the visibility and marketability of college sports. The establishment of these networks has not only transformed the financial landscape but has also enhanced fan engagement, granting unprecedented access to a plethora of athletic events.

The interplay between market dynamics and media roles in college sports continues to evolve, particularly with the expansion of digital platforms. The rise of online streaming services has shattered traditional geographic barriers, enabling smaller programs to broadcast their games to a global audience. This access has redefined fan engagement, allowing supporters to follow their teams irrespective of location. While this has opened up new revenue streams and marketing opportunities, it has also introduced heightened competition for viewership and brand loyalty, as institutions now vie for attention in an increasingly crowded digital marketplace.

Digital Disruption and Competitive Balance

The proliferation of digital platforms in the broadcasting of college sports has brought both opportunities and challenges. On one hand, these platforms have facilitated a more engaged and interactive fan experience. Social media, for example, allows for real-time engagement between teams and their supporters, creating a dynamic environment that traditional media could not offer. On the other hand, the sheer volume of content available online has ushered in a fiercely competitive environment. Colleges and universities must now differentiate their offerings and find innovative ways to capture and retain fan interest in a market where consumers are inundated with choices.

This competition extends beyond just viewership. It encompasses the battle for talent, as student-athletes consider the visibility and branding opportunities provided by various programs. The digital and media space can influence recruiting, with high-profile media exposure often translating into an appealing prospect for potential recruits.

Fiscal Implications and Ethical Considerations

The fiscal implications of media rights and digital platforms in college sports are profound. The revenue generated from broadcasting deals and digital engagements can finance facility upgrades, bolster coaching staff salaries, and enhance overall athletic program quality. However, as commercial revenues surge, so too do ethical considerations. Questions arise about the impact of commercial pressures on the educational values that college sports purport to uphold. The debate intensifies when media obligations conflict with academic schedules, or when the commercialization of college sports appears to overshadow their educational mission.

In sum, the market dynamics and the role of media in college sports represent a multifaceted and evolving domain. Media rights agreements have long been a significant source of income, and the advent of digital platforms has expanded the reach and engagement of college sports programs. Yet, with these financial opportunities come new challenges and ethical debates, ensuring that the marketplace of college sports remains a complex and dynamic sector within higher education.

Discussion Questions

- How does the emotional investment of stakeholders in college sports impact financial decisions and business strategies?
- Identify ways in which this emotional connection can be both a strength and a vulnerability for college athletic programs.
- What are the challenges of maintaining a college's educational values and mission in the face of increasing commercial pressures in college sports?
- In light of recent debates on athlete compensation, how might changes in regulations transform the business model of college sports?
- How have media rights agreements transformed the financial landscape of college sports?
- What are the potential benefits and challenges that digital platforms pose for the business of college sports?
- How can college sports maintain their traditional values in an increasingly commercialized environment?
- Discuss the role of tradition in the branding and marketing strategies of college athletic programs.

Case Study 2.1: The Dual Economics of College Sports

College sports represent a unique business model, situated at the crossroads of higher education and high-stakes entertainment. Unlike their professional counterparts, collegiate teams are not standalone entities but are integral components of their academic institutions. Their success on the field is deeply intertwined with their university's reputation, enrollment, and alumni relations. This case study aims to explore how college sports function as a business, driving value for their institutions while also serving as a powerful medium for community engagement and school spirit.

The Event

Consider a scenario where a mid-sized university makes an unprecedented run in a national basketball tournament. With each victory, the school gains national exposure, merchandise sales skyrocket, and applications for admission see a significant spike. The basketball program, once a modest operation, is now in the spotlight, negotiating substantial media rights deals and attracting high-profile sponsors. This sudden surge in attention brings financial gains but also challenges the university's commitment to academic excellence and its educational mission.

The Impact

- Financial Windfall: The university experiences a substantial increase in revenue from merchandise, ticket sales, and sponsorships. This influx of capital allows for investments in facilities, academic programs, and recruitment efforts.
- Elevated Profile: National exposure brings the university into the limelight, potentially increasing the quantity and quality of student applications and expanding its alumni donor base.
- Mission vs. Market: With the new-found success and commercial opportunities, the university grapples with maintaining a balance between exploiting the financial opportunities presented by a successful sports program and adhering to its primary mission of education and personal development.

Discussion

- How should the university manage its new financial resources to benefit both the athletic department and the institution's broader academic mission?
- In what ways might the commercial success of the basketball program conflict with the university's educational values? What measures can be taken to ensure that the student-athlete's academic and personal development remains a priority?

- Considering the cyclical nature of sports success, how can the university leverage its current success for long-term growth and stability, both in athletics and academics?

Case Study 2.2: The Sponsorship Gamble of Sports Programs

A mid-tier university's athletic department, known for its distinguished women's soccer team, faced financial constraints that threatened the continuation of several sports programs. The department decided to focus on leveraging the women's soccer team's success to secure a substantial sponsorship deal that would provide the financial stability needed to support other programs. The challenge was to find a sponsor who aligned with the university's values and to structure a deal that would benefit both parties without compromising the integrity of the university and its athletes.

The Event
The university entered into negotiations with a well-known energy drink company, which offered a lucrative sponsorship deal. The energy drink market was controversial due to health concerns, especially for young consumers, but the financial offer was significantly higher than any other sponsorship prospect. The proposed deal included renaming the soccer stadium, prominent logos on team kits, and direct marketing access to students on campus.

The Impact
The deal sparked intense debate within the university community. Proponents highlighted the financial benefits, increased exposure for the women's soccer team, and the potential for enhanced recruitment. Opponents raised concerns about promoting unhealthy products to students, the commercialization of college sports, and the potential for the deal to distract from the educational mission of the institution.

Discussion
- Evaluate the ethical considerations the university must balance when entering a sponsorship deal with potential health implications for students.
- Discuss the impact of financial pressures on decision-making within university sports programs.
- Consider the implications for the university's reputation and student-athlete welfare when partnering with controversial sponsors.
- Explore alternative strategies for raising funds without compromising the university's values or the health of its students.
- Assess how the sponsorship could affect the student body's perception of the athletic department and the university as a whole.

Chapter 3
History of the NCAA and College Sport Governance

The National Collegiate Athletic Association (NCAA) has played a pivotal role in shaping the landscape of college sports in the United States. Its formation, evolution, and the governance of collegiate athletics reflect a rich tapestry of change, challenge, and innovation that continue to influence the direction and operation of college sports today.

Upon successful completion of this unit, students will be able to:

- Understand and articulate the social and economic significance of modern intercollegiate athletics within the broader societal context.
- Recount the historical progression and transformative events in intercollegiate sport from its inception in 1852 to the current era.
- Assess the jurisdiction and influence of various governing bodies in intercollegiate athletics, including the NCAA, NAIA, and NJCAA.
- Identify and differentiate the salient features of NCAA Division I, II, and III athletic programs, and distinguish between the Football Bowl Subdivision (FBS) and Football Championship Subdivision (FCS) within Division I.
- Construct a mental model of the NCAA's organizational framework and discern how this structure affects the organization's policymaking and operations.
- Enumerate the myriad career paths available within the realm of intercollegiate athletics and specify the competencies necessary for professional success in these roles.

Formation and Early Years

At the dawn of the 20th century, the landscape of college sports was a far cry from the structured and regulated environment we know today. Collegiate football, which would become a cornerstone of American sports culture, was in a state of disarray, with rules that were as varied as they were vague. The consequence was a sport that, while popular, was perilously violent and unregulated. It was not uncommon for the season to culminate with numerous serious injuries and, tragically, fatalities among the young athletes. This perilous state of affairs caught the attention of none other than President Theodore Roosevelt, an ardent advocate for the "strenuous life" but also a proponent of fair play and safety. In 1905, following a particularly brutal year that resulted in eighteen deaths, he summoned college leaders to the White House and implored them to reform football.

Heeding the President's call, sixty-two colleges and universities came together to form the Intercollegiate Athletic Association of the United States (IAAUS) in December 1906, marking a pivotal moment in the history of college sports. The IAAUS, which would be renamed the National Collegiate Athletic Association (NCAA) in 1910, had a clear and noble mandate: to protect the young men who played the game and to imbue the sport with a sense of fairness and order.
The NCAA's initial efforts were primarily focused on rule changes in football to eliminate the roughest aspects of the game. They introduced measures such as the legalization of the forward pass, a ten-yard requirement for first downs, and a ban on mass formation plays, which significantly reduced injuries. But the NCAA's influence did not stop at rule adjustments; it slowly started to reshape the landscape of college sports altogether.

Initially operating as a voluntary association, the NCAA's role in the early years was more advisory than authoritative. It made recommendations for safety measures and worked to create a standardized set of rules that could be uniformly adopted. This period was characterized by the organization's collaborative efforts to prioritize the well-being of student-athletes, a foundational principle that remains at its core to this day.

As the NCAA's influence expanded, so too did its remit. By the 1920s, the association had begun to oversee not just football but other collegiate sports as well. It became the chief custodian of college athletics, a role that involved far more than merely sanctioning games. The NCAA started to address broader issues such as eligibility—setting standards for who could compete in college sports—and scholarships, laying down rules on financial aid for athletes.

A crucial part of the NCAA's burgeoning responsibility was the maintenance of amateur status for student-athletes. As the popularity of college sports grew, so did the stakes, with commercial interests increasingly infringing on the amateur ethos that college sports were built on. The NCAA found itself at the intersection of preserving this ethos while also adapting to the changing landscape where sports were becoming a more central part of the college experience and, indeed, the economic model of institutions.

As the NCAA moved through the 20th century, it continued to adapt and evolve. The organization that began as a means to reform a single sport had become the definitive authority over collegiate athletics, shaping the policies that governed the athletic and academic lives of student-athletes and influencing the culture and finances of the institutions it served. Its journey from a rudimentary rule-making assembly to a comprehensive regulatory body is a testament to the enduring complexity and importance of college sports in American life.

Expansion and Professionalization

The trajectory of the NCAA's growth during the mid-20th century is reflective of the broader ascension of college sports from campus pastimes to spectacles of national significance. As the allure of college sports burgeoned, so too did the authority and the operational purview of the NCAA. The association's mandate expanded beyond its original scope as it began to shape the character of collegiate athletics, standardizing practices, and fostering a competitive environment that resonated across the country.

The pivotal moment in this trajectory came in 1952 when the NCAA secured its first television contract for college football. This deal was not just a financial boon; it symbolized a new epoch wherein media rights emerged as a central pillar of revenue generation for the association and its member institutions. The games that were once confined to college campuses and local communities were now broadcast into living rooms nationwide, amplifying the reach of college sports and embedding them into the fabric of American culture.

With the expansion into national media, the NCAA's stewardship faced new challenges. The association found itself navigating the tenuous line between maintaining the amateur status of student-athletes—a cornerstone of collegiate athletics—and embracing the professionalism that came with the burgeoning commercial potential of the sports. As college football and later basketball became fixtures on television screens, the revenues grew exponentially, prompting debates over the definition and preservation of amateurism in an increasingly professionalized environment.

The NCAA responded to these challenges by fortifying its regulatory framework, establishing stringent eligibility standards aimed at ensuring that athletes remained amateurs in the truest sense. It orchestrated national championships, elevating the profile and the stakes of college sports, and further entrenching its position as the arbiter of collegiate athletics. However, this consolidation of power was not without its detractors. The organization came under scrutiny for what many perceived as an overreach of its regulatory powers and for not adequately compensating the very athletes who contributed to the burgeoning financial success of college sports.

This period marked a crescendo of sorts, where the commercial potential of college sports was realized and capitalized upon, setting the stage for the multimillion-dollar industry that collegiate athletics is today. Yet, it also underscored an inherent conflict within the NCAA's model—a conflict between the amateur spirit that defined the participation of student-athletes and the professional commercialism that now underscored the administration of college sports. This paradox would continue to animate the discourse surrounding the NCAA and shape the evolution of its policies and practices in the decades to follow.

Challenges and Controversies

The chronicle of the NCAA is punctuated by a series of legal and ethical challenges, each serving as a catalyst for change within the organization and the broader realm of college sports. Throughout its storied past, the NCAA has repeatedly found itself at the epicenter of controversy, necessitating a delicate balance between safeguarding the integrity of college sports and evolving to meet the demands of a changing legal and social landscape.

A watershed moment in the NCAA's history arrived in 1984 with the landmark Supreme Court decision in NCAA v. Board of Regents of the University of Oklahoma. This pivotal case resulted in the NCAA losing its exclusive control over television broadcast rights for football. Prior to this, the NCAA had a monopoly on television contracts, deciding which games were televised, when, and how often. The Supreme Court's ruling fundamentally altered the economic landscape of college football, ushering in an era of individual conferences and schools negotiating their own television contracts. This not only democratized the broadcasting of games but also led to an explosion of revenue for successful athletic programs, fundamentally changing the business model of college sports.

The ramifications of this decision are evident in today's college sports environment, where television rights serve as the financial lifeblood for many athletic programs. The influx of broadcast money has financed the escalating arms race in facilities, salaries, and recruiting that characterizes modern college athletics. However, with this financial windfall, the debate over the role and rights of student-athletes intensified, leading to a sustained discourse on the notion of amateurism and what it means to be a student-athlete.

In parallel with these legal battles, the NCAA has had to grapple with critical issues of social justice and equity. The passage of Title IX in 1972 was a significant stride forward in gender equity in college sports. This federal law mandated equal opportunities for men and women in all educational programs that receive federal funding, including athletics. The implementation of Title IX forced colleges and universities, and by extension the NCAA, to reassess and restructure their athletic programs to ensure compliance. This often resulted in the expansion of women's sports programs and increased investment in women's athletics, reshaping the collegiate athletic environment.

Furthermore, the discourse surrounding the compensation of student-athletes gained momentum with cases like that of Ed O'Bannon, a former UCLA basketball player who filed a lawsuit challenging the NCAA's use of the images of former student-athletes for commercial purposes without compensation. The case highlighted the growing discontent with NCAA regulations that restrict athlete compensation, especially in light of the increasing revenues generated from college sports. This led to subsequent rulings that have begun to dismantle the NCAA's longstanding amateurism rules, culminating in the recent allowance for student-athletes to profit from their name, image, and likeness (NIL) rights.

These challenges and legal milestones reflect a history of the NCAA that is marked by adaptation and resistance, struggle, and progress. As the NCAA continues to navigate the complex interplay between its foundational principles and the realities of the contemporary sports landscape, it stands as a testament to the enduring complexity of governing a system that is, at its heart, both an educational endeavor and a commercial juggernaut.

Recent Developments and Future Directions

In the face of mounting criticism, the NCAA has attempted to reform itself, instituting measures to prioritize academic performance and to grant more autonomy to the so-called Power Five conferences. However, these reforms have often been seen as too little, too late. The NCAA's ability to govern has been further complicated by changes in public sentiment, legislative actions, and the courts, challenging the association's traditional stance on amateurism and raising questions about its future role in the governance of college sports.

The history of the NCAA is a testament to its resilience and capacity to adapt amidst the ever-changing landscape of collegiate athletics. Starting as a modest endeavor to ensure player safety and fair competition, the NCAA has grown into a commanding presence within college sports. Legal battles, such as the 1984 Supreme Court ruling that redefined media rights, have been significant in this evolution, expanding the economic horizons of athletic programs. Additionally, legislative landmarks like Title IX have driven the NCAA to uphold gender equity, demonstrating its role in fostering a more inclusive environment.

The debate over student-athlete compensation, particularly highlighted by the Ed O'Bannon case, has intensified discussions on the commercialization of college sports and the NCAA's conception of amateurism. With the recent shift toward recognizing the NIL rights of student-athletes, the NCAA's policies and their alignment with the organization's core values have come under increasing scrutiny. These controversies underscore the NCAA's complex role as a regulator of a system that straddles educational objectives and the competitive, commercial nature of modern sports.

Moving into the future, the NCAA finds itself at a crossroads, challenged to maintain its relevance and authority as the protector of student-athletes and the integrity of college sports. It faces the task of harmonizing the commercial realities of the industry with the academic and developmental mission of collegiate athletics. How the NCAA responds to these challenges, adapting its policies to the demands of an industry in flux while preserving the student-athlete experience, will shape its identity and legacy in the years to come.

Discussion Questions

- How did the mission and minimum standards set by the NCAA at its inception address the violence and safety concerns in college sports during the early 20th century?
- Discuss the impact of the NCAA's first television contract with NBC in 1952. How did this contract set a precedent for the commercialization of college sports?
- Examine the NCAA's role in enforcing amateurism rules. How did the scandal involving Southern Methodist University in the 1980s

highlight the challenges faced by the NCAA in maintaining amateur status among student-athletes?

- In what ways has the evolution of media rights agreements affected the NCAA's governance of college sports?
- How do historical events such as the SMU scandal inform current debates about compensating student-athletes? What lessons can be drawn from past enforcement efforts by the NCAA?
- What measures can the NCAA implement to balance commercial interests and the educational values it seeks to uphold?

Case Study 3.1: The Challenges of Institutional Control in NCAA Governance

The NCAA, established in 1906, has evolved from a body intent on reforming college football to prevent injuries and fatalities to a powerful organization overseeing collegiate athletics. It's not a government agency but a collective of educational institutions with significant independence in enforcing its policies, aiming to keep college sports as an integral part of the education system. However, with the growing commercialization of college sports and significant financial stakes involved, challenges in maintaining integrity and institutional control have become more pronounced.

The Event
St. Bonaventure University, a member of the NCAA, faced a severe challenge to its institutional control over the eligibility and conduct of its men's basketball program. A student-athlete's eligibility was in question due to his academic background, and the university's president and an assistant basketball coach (who was the president's son) bypassed proper channels to declare the student eligible. They even altered his academic records to ensure his continued participation in games, directly contradicting NCAA guidelines.

The Impact
The breakdown in institutional control at St. Bonaventure resulted in the NCAA imposing a three-year probation on the school's athletic programs. The men's basketball team was barred from post-season competition, and there were restrictions placed on recruitment. Additionally, this led to a restructuring of the university's governance system. High-profile resignations followed, including those of the president, athletic director, and the basketball coaching staff, indicating the gravity of the institutional failures and the severe consequences that can ensue.

Discussion
- How can colleges and universities ensure that the pursuit of athletic success does not compromise academic integrity and compliance with NCAA regulations?
- What mechanisms can the NCAA implement to more effectively monitor and maintain institutional control within its member organizations?
- Considering the financial pressures and incentives in college sports, what steps can be taken to balance commercial success with the educational mission of collegiate athletics?
- In light of the St. Bonaventure case, discuss the ethical responsibilities of university leadership in upholding NCAA standards and protecting the welfare of student-athletes.

Case Study 3.2: NCAA Balancing Act

The NCAA's inception aimed to tackle the violent and hazardous nature of early 20th-century college football. However, limited enforcement powers and reluctance from football powerhouses to relinquish control meant the NCAA began with little real influence. By 1952, the NCAA found its stride, executing its first television contract under executive director Walter Byers, thus beginning its rise to prominence.

The Event
The NCAA's significant leap forward came with their ability to control and sell television rights for college football, starting a trajectory of lucrative deals that shaped the financial landscape of college sports. However, this central control didn't go unchallenged. Schools with larger followings, such as the University of Oklahoma and the University of Georgia, saw this as a limitation on potential earnings. This led to the formation of the College Football Association and a landmark 1984 U.S. Supreme Court decision that ruled the NCAA's TV contracts violated antitrust laws.

The Impact
The aftermath of the Supreme Court decision drastically changed the economics of college sports, decentralizing media rights and inflating revenues. Moreover, the NCAA's enforcement of amateurism rules became a focal point, particularly with the Southern Methodist University scandal in the 1980s, resulting in the infamous "death penalty." These events solidified the NCAA's regulatory role in intercollegiate athletics, setting a precedent for handling violations and financial control.

Discussion

- How did the centralization of television rights by the NCAA initially benefit the organization and its member institutions?
- In what ways did the 1984 Supreme Court decision reshape the financial model of college sports?
- Consider the ethical implications of the NCAA's strict enforcement of amateurism rules while securing billion-dollar media contracts.
- Discuss the long-term effects of the NCAA's "death penalty" on institutional compliance and the overall college athletic culture.
- Reflect on the balance between financial growth and maintaining amateurism within college sports. How should the NCAA navigate this dichotomy?

Chapter 4
Governance in Collegiate Athletics

In the complex landscape of collegiate athletics, the governance structure plays a critical role in ensuring fairness, equity, and integrity across all levels of competition. This chapter delves into the intricate governance mechanisms of collegiate sports in the United States, focusing on the major national governing bodies: the National Collegiate Athletic Association (NCAA), the National Association of Intercollegiate Athletics (NAIA), the United States Collegiate Athletic Association (USCAA), the National Christian College Athletic Association (NCCAA), the National Junior College Athletic Association (NJCAA), and the Canadian Collegiate Athletic Association (CCAA).

Upon successful completion of this unit, students will be able to:

- Identify the primary functions, organizational structures, and unique characteristics of the NCAA, NAIA, USCAA, NCCAA, NJCAA, and CCAA and explain how each contributes to the governance of collegiate athletics.
- Evaluate how the NCAA's Principles of Conduct for Intercollegiate Athletics influence the behavior and policies of institutions, ensuring integrity, fairness, and the welfare of student-athletes, and promoting a balance between athletics, academics, and social experiences.
- Describe the operational strategies employed by the NCAA, NAIA, USCAA, NCCAA, NJCAA, and CCAA to serve their stakeholders, including student-athletes, member institutions, coaches, and the community, highlighting how each body fulfills its mission within the collegiate sports ecosystem.
- Utilize knowledge of governance structures and principles to analyze real-world case studies or hypothetical scenarios within collegiate athletics, focusing on decision-making processes, ethical considerations, and compliance with governing body regulations.

The Structure of National Governing Bodies in Collegiate Athletics

The structure of national governing bodies in collegiate athletics includes organizations like the NCAA, NAIA, NJCAA, and CCAA, each serving diverse institutions across North America. These bodies oversee college sports, with specific associations like the USCAA and NCCAA focusing on smaller or faith-based colleges. Collectively, they ensure a wide range of athletic and academic opportunities for student-athletes.

National Collegiate Athletic Association (NCAA)

The NCAA, as a comprehensive governing body, divides its member institutions into three distinct classifications based on various criteria that impact the level of competition, the resources available to athletes, and the institution's commitment to athletics. Understanding the differences between NCAA Division I, II, and III is essential for stakeholders ranging from student-athletes to administrators, as these distinctions affect not only the athletic experience but also the academic and community environments of the institutions.

Division I is the most visible and competitive tier within the NCAA structure, representing the largest universities with the biggest athletic budgets. These institutions often have greater resources to allocate towards recruiting top-tier talent, providing state-of-the-art facilities, and offering a wide array of athletic scholarships. Academic progress and eligibility standards in Division I are stringent, reflecting the high stakes of maintaining both athletic and academic performance. Division I schools are typically larger universities with robust support systems for athletes, including comprehensive coaching staff, sports medicine, and academic services. They are the most likely to be featured in televised sports, generate significant revenue from athletics (especially in high-profile sports like football and basketball), and have the highest attendance rates for events. The expectation for competitiveness in Division I is unmatched, often leading to a more rigorous demand on the student-athletes' time for training, practice, and travel.

Division II serves as a middle ground in the NCAA structure, providing a balance between athletic competition and academic rigor. While still competitive, Division II focuses on a more balanced college experience, where student-athletes are encouraged to engage with their campus and surrounding community. Institutions in Division II are typically smaller than those in Division I and offer fewer athletic scholarships. The division prides itself on its "Life in the Balance" philosophy, which emphasizes comprehensive learning experiences over athletic achievements alone. Student-athletes are expected to maintain good academic standing and are encouraged to participate in community and campus life outside of their sport.

Division III represents the largest number of NCAA institutions and places the primary focus on the overall collegiate experience of the student-athlete. This division strictly prohibits the offering of athletic scholarships, underlining its dedication to the amateurism and educational quality of the student-athletes' experiences. Institutions in Division III are often smaller colleges and universities that value the traditional ideals of collegiate sport. Student-athletes in Division III are expected to prioritize their academic work, with athletic participation seen as an important, but secondary, part of the college experience. The emphasis is on personal growth, academic excellence, and the development of leadership and community skills.

National Association of Intercollegiate Athletics (NAIA)

The National Association of Intercollegiate Athletics (NAIA) represents an alternative approach to collegiate sports governance, one that is particularly suited to smaller colleges and universities that may not have the vast resources of larger NCAA institutions. By emphasizing a student-centered experience, the NAIA offers an environment where athletic participation is integral to the educational journey, but not at the expense of character and academic success.

The NAIA's model creates a triad of priorities, each holding equal weight in the development of its student-athletes. This triad—athletics, academics, and character—forms the essence of the NAIA's philosophy. While competition remains a pivotal aspect of the student-athlete experience, it does not overshadow academic responsibilities or the cultivation of character. This balance ensures that NAIA athletes can commit fully to their sport without compromising their education or personal development.

In contrast to the NCAA's highly commercialized and competitive nature, particularly at the Division I level, the NAIA's more holistic approach fosters environments where athletic programs serve as an extension of the educational mission rather than a separate entity. The NAIA's smaller institutional memberships often lead to close-knit communities where individual student-athletes can stand out and make significant contributions, not just within their teams but also within the broader college community.

The NAIA's distinctive approach to collegiate athletics governance positions it as an appealing option for smaller colleges and universities that value a well-balanced collegiate experience. By putting a premium on character development, academic success, and meaningful athletic participation, the NAIA offers a compelling alternative that aligns the goals of higher education with the passionate pursuit of athletic excellence.

United States Collegiate Athletic Association (USCAA)

The United States Collegiate Athletic Association (USCAA), with its membership primarily based in the northeastern United States, is the smallest intercollegiate athletic national organization in the nation, boasting around 80 member institutions which include both two-year and four-year colleges. Unlike larger associations, the USCAA permits dual membership, allowing institutions to be part of the NAIA, NJCAA, and NCAA Division III simultaneously. The USCAA's history traces back to its founding in 1966 as the National Little College Athletic Association, eventually evolving into its current form in 2001. With the ethos of providing 'wholesome athletic competition' to small colleges, the USCAA has established a constitution which promotes the comprehensive development of student-athletes and espouses values such as integrity, leadership, scholarship, and a balanced life. By offering an equitable platform for competition, the USCAA's main goal is to facilitate athletic engagements that contribute positively to the educational experiences of its participants.

National Christian College Athletic Association (NCCAA)

The National Christian College Athletic Association (NCCAA) was established in 1968, beginning with a men's basketball tournament in Detroit, Michigan, and currently has its national office in Greenville, South Carolina. With a mission that intertwines athletic competition with Christian values, the NCCAA stands distinct as a national and international governing body. It offers championships in 18 men's and women's sports across two divisional classifications and includes approximately 110 institutions across 28 states and two Canadian provinces.

The NCCAA's philosophy emphasizes that athletics serve a more significant end, valuing the student-athlete's personal growth and character development over win-loss records and championships. It promotes the idea that athletic participation at a Christian liberal arts or Bible college is not just about competition but a unique experience that prepares individuals for a life of meaningful work and service. The NCCAA believes that the process of competing is as crucial as the outcomes and that participation in sports is a vital aspect of learning discipline, teamwork, leadership, and mutual respect.

Furthermore, the NCCAA adopts an innovative stance in its operations, allowing member schools to maintain affiliations with other associations for scheduling purposes, ensuring logistical viability. This flexibility exemplifies the NCCAA's commitment to its student-athletes and member institutions, promoting athletic competition alongside spiritual and character development. The association also actively engages in outreach and ministry, reinforcing the role of athletics as a growth process aligning with Christian teachings and principles. Through this multifaceted approach, the NCCAA strives to enhance the collegiate athletic experience, integrating sportsmanship and fellowship with a Christian worldview.

National Junior College Athletic Association (NJCAA)

The National Junior College Athletic Association (NJCAA) plays a pivotal role in the athletic and academic lives of student-athletes at two-year colleges. By sponsoring championships in 13 men's and 13 women's sports across three divisions, the NJCAA not only fosters competition but also addresses the financial aspect of college sports. Each division corresponds to a level of athletics-related financial aid that schools can offer, from comprehensive scholarships in Division I to no athletic aid in Division III. This structure aims to balance the playing field and provide equitable opportunities in alignment with the educational missions of member colleges.

The NJCAA stands as a distinct entity that champions the development of student-athletes who may hail from both conventional and non-traditional backgrounds. Its mission focuses on encouraging athletic participation that is consistent with the educational objectives of the member institutions. For many student-athletes, the NJCAA serves as an instrumental platform that allows them to pursue academic and athletic excellence with the prospect of transferring to four-year institutions to continue their endeavors. Emphasizing its unique place in the intercollegiate athletic landscape, the NJCAA offers a gateway to further advancement for those who may face familial, economic, or other barriers in their academic and athletic pursuits.

Canadian Collegiate Athletic Association (CCAA)

The Canadian Collegiate Athletic Association (CCAA) is the national body overseeing college sports in Canada, distinct from its American counterpart, the NCAA. Formed in 1974, it emphasizes a balance between academics and athletics, offering fewer athletic scholarships compared to the NCAA. It governs sports through regional associations across Canada without the divisional tiers found in the NCAA, and student-athletes have a maximum of five years of eligibility. The CCAA is known for a less intense but competitive level of sports participation, focusing more on student development than on professional sports pathways. The sports offered vary, reflecting each country's sporting preferences, with sports like Canadian football being more prominent in the CCAA.

The CCAA supports student-athletes with national championships, awards, and recognition programs across nine provinces, governed by six regional conferences. These include the PACWEST in British Columbia, ACAC in Alberta and Saskatchewan, MCAC in Manitoba, OCAA in Ontario, RSEQ in Québec, and ACAA in Atlantic Canada. The organization values fair play, sportsmanship, and respect, contributing to the development of collegiate sports in Canada while also focusing on academic success and inclusivity, offering a complete educational and athletic experience to its members.

NCAA's Principles of Conduct and Organizational Fulfillment

The NCAA's Principles of Conduct for Intercollegiate Athletics are established to assure that the association and its member institutions operate in alignment with key ethical standards and values. The principles are grounded in the organization's constitution and detailed in Article 2, outlining the rationale for all NCAA legislation. They form the underpinning of the NCAA's operational guidelines, ensuring programs are in harmony with the organization's overall mission and objectives.

- Principle of Institutional Control and Responsibility: This principle mandates that each NCAA member institution must maintain control over its athletics program in compliance with NCAA rules. The responsibility for such control ultimately resides with the institution's president, extending to all associated with the athletic interests of the institution.
- Principle of Student-Athlete Well-Being: Emphasizes that intercollegiate athletic programs must operate to protect and enhance the physical and educational welfare of student-athletes. This includes maintaining an environment that values cultural diversity and gender equity, ensuring health and safety, fostering a positive coach-athlete relationship, and providing fairness and honesty in administrative relations.
- Principle of Gender Equity: Requires compliance with federal and state gender equity laws, including Title IX. It aims to ensure that the NCAA does not enact legislation that impedes these laws and that NCAA activities are free of gender bias.
- Principle of Sportsmanship and Ethical Conduct: Stresses that

individuals within athletic departments must adhere to core values such as respect, fairness, civility, honesty, and responsibility. These values should reflect in both on-field performance and the broader administrative context, aligning with the educational mission of the institution.

- Principle of Sound Academic Standards: Asserts that intercollegiate athletics should be an integral part of the educational program and that student-athletes must be genuine members of the student body, adhering to the same academic standards and progress requirements.
- Principle of Nondiscrimination: The NCAA is dedicated to promoting respect and sensitivity for the dignity of every person, avoiding discrimination in its governance policies, educational programs, and employment policies. This extends to individual athletic departments, which must create policies that support this principle.
- Principle of Diversity within Governance Structures: Advocates for ethnic and gender diversity within the NCAA's governance and administrative structures, emphasizing the need for representation of historically underrepresented groups.
- Principle of Rules Compliance: Every member institution is committed to adhering to NCAA rules and regulations and is responsible for monitoring and reporting compliance, as well as fully cooperating with any investigations.
- Principle of Amateurism: This principle asserts that student-athletes must be amateurs, motivated by education and the benefits derived from athletic participation. The NCAA strives to distinguish clearly between intercollegiate and professional sports, protecting student-athletes from commercial exploitation.

The application of these principles reflects the NCAA's commitment to ensuring that its member institutions and the broader intercollegiate athletics community operate in a manner that is fair, ethical, and respectful of all individuals involved. This includes promoting integrity, equity, academic excellence, and inclusiveness in all facets of intercollegiate athletics management and governance.

Operational Modalities and Stakeholder Service

Each national governing body operates with distinct modalities to serve its stakeholders, including student-athletes, institutions, coaches, and communities. National governing bodies like the NCAA have established complex governance structures to maintain a fair and supportive environment for all stakeholders. This involves creating legislative processes, enforcement programs, and educational initiatives that align with the body's mission and principles. The NCAA's comprehensive structure is designed to deliver value to participants, uphold integrity, ensure equity and foster academic excellence. On the other hand, organizations such as the NAIA, USCAA, NCCAA, and NJCAA, though varying in size and reach, similarly prioritize the welfare and advancement of student-athletes. They provide competitive platforms and developmental opportunities, ensuring their operations are in sync with their core objectives and mission statements. These organizations conduct periodic audits, reviews, and opinion surveys with user groups and potential consumers to guide their marketing, public relations strategies, and program adjustments.

The operational modalities adopted by these bodies demonstrate a commitment to continuous improvement, recognizing the dynamic nature of intercollegiate athletics. Encouraging and rewarding staff for innovative ideas, and adapting to the evolving landscape of sports management, they work to ensure that no stakeholder feels marginalized. Each organization's mission and objectives, reflecting the needs and desires of current and potential participants, form the bedrock of their operational ethos, guiding their marketing processes and strategic initiatives. Thus, through their distinct operational modalities and focus on stakeholder service, national governing bodies in collegiate athletics play a pivotal role in shaping the experience of student-athletes and the broader community engaged in sports at the collegiate level.

Discussion Questions

- How do the structures and operations of the NCAA, NAIA, USCAA, NCCAA, and NJCAA differ, and what implications do these differences have for the governance of collegiate athletics?
- In what ways do the NCAA's Principles of Conduct influence the behavior and decision-making of its member institutions, and how do they contribute to the broader goals of collegiate athletics?
- How do national governing bodies like the NCAA and NAIA balance competitive athletics with academic achievement and personal development, and what challenges do they face in this endeavor?
- How do factors such as commercialization, legal challenges, and ethical considerations affect the governance and operations of collegiate athletic organizations?
- Considering the current landscape of collegiate athletics, what strategies might governing bodies employ to enhance governance, ensure athlete welfare, and address contemporary challenges?
- How do governing bodies address issues of diversity, equity, and inclusion within collegiate athletics, and what more can be done to promote an inclusive environment for all participants?

Case Study 4.1: Implementation of NCAA's Principles of Conduct

The National Collegiate Athletic Association (NCAA) upholds a set of principles that guide the conduct of intercollegiate athletics. These principles are designed to support fairness, sportsmanship, and the well-being of student-athletes and form the backbone of the NCAA's governance system.

The Event

A Division II college faced scrutiny after several student-athletes reported feeling pressure to prioritize sports over academics. This initiated an audit to assess the institution's adherence to the NCAA's Principles of Conduct, particularly focusing on institutional control and responsibility, student-athlete well-being, and sound academic standards.

The Impact

The audit revealed gaps in the college's policies and practices, including inadequate academic support for student-athletes and a culture that implicitly encouraged athletic success over educational achievements. The findings led to widespread reform within the athletic department, including the introduction of mandatory academic workshops and adjusted training schedules to reduce conflicts with academics.

Discussion

- How should institutions balance athletic success with academic integrity, and what strategies could be put in place to ensure adherence to the NCAA's Principles of Conduct?
- In what ways can institutions foster an environment that better balances the demands of athletics and academics for student-athletes?
- What mechanisms can be put in place to ensure institutions remain accountable to the NCAA's Principles of Conduct?
- How can institutional leaders effect cultural change within their athletics departments to prioritize academic integrity?
- What are the long-term implications for institutions that fail to adhere to the NCAA's Principles of Conduct, both from an ethical and a regulatory standpoint?

Case Study 4.2: NJCAA's Role in Shaping Two-Year College Athletics

The National Junior College Athletic Association (NJCAA) is central to the world of two-year college athletics, providing oversight and opportunities for student-athletes to compete while pursuing academic qualifications. With a varied range of sponsored sports and divisions based on financial aid capabilities, the NJCAA aligns athletic competition with educational ambitions.

The Event

A two-year college in a rural area was struggling to attract talent and retain student-athletes due to financial constraints and limited exposure. The NJCAA stepped in to reassess the institution's athletic program, focusing on equitable opportunities and financial aid options. The association's intervention led to the restructuring of athletic scholarships and a marketing initiative aimed at highlighting the college's unique academic and athletic offerings.

The Impact

The college saw a significant uptick in student-athlete enrollment and retention. Athletes benefited from more balanced support between their academic pursuits and athletic endeavors, leading to an increase in transfer rates to four-year institutions. The college also received recognition for its commitment to diversity and gender equity, further aligning with NJCAA's principles.

Discussion

- How can two-year colleges under the NJCAA better support the dual objectives of their student-athletes in academics and sports?
- What strategies can the NJCAA implement to help member colleges in less affluent areas improve their athletic programs while ensuring financial sustainability?
- How does the NJCAA ensure that its member institutions maintain a commitment to diversity, equity, and inclusion in their athletic programs?
- How can the NJCAA facilitate smoother transitions for student-athletes moving from two-year colleges to four-year institutions?
- What approaches can two-year colleges take to improve their visibility and attractiveness to prospective student-athletes within the NJCAA framework?

Chapter 5
Organization of the NCAA

The National Collegiate Athletic Association (NCAA) stands as a cornerstone in the realm of college athletics, administering rules and regulations that shape the structure and conduct of intercollegiate sports in the United States. The organization's influence stretches across three divisions (I, II, and III), each characterized by its own unique set of standards and requirements. This chapter delves into the organization of the NCAA, focusing particularly on the intricate workings of an NCAA Division I athletic department, which represents the zenith in terms of athletic competition, financial budgets, and visibility within the collegiate sports landscape.

Upon successful completion of this unit, students will be able to:

- Identify the core functions and structure of the NCAA and explain how these influence the operation of collegiate athletic departments.
- Assess the roles and responsibilities of an Athletic Director (AD), considering the demands of leadership and administration in collegiate sports.
- Analyze the importance of compliance within the NCAA structure and the impact of adherence to its regulations on the integrity of athletic programs.
- Evaluate the significance of academic support services and sports medicine in promoting student-athlete well-being and academic success.
- Discuss the role of fundraising and development in enhancing the sustainability and growth of collegiate athletic departments.
- Critique the challenges and opportunities inherent in the management of NCAA athletic departments, particularly in light of financial pressures and the evolving landscape of collegiate athletics.

The NCAA: An Overview

Established in 1906, the NCAA was founded to safeguard student-athletes and ensure that college athletics remain a valuable component of the educational experience. Over the years, it has evolved into a complex entity that oversees numerous sports across hundreds of institutions. Its primary responsibilities include managing national championships, enforcing compliance with sportsmanship and academic standards, and distributing revenue to support student-athletes' educational pursuits.

Structure and Governance

The NCAA is structured into three divisions to provide a fair and equitable competitive environment that matches the diverse missions and resources of its member institutions. These divisions are:

- Division I: Known for its high-profile athletics programs, Division I institutions must sponsor at least seven sports for men and seven for women (or six for men and eight for women). These schools often have larger budgets, more athletic scholarships, and more extensive facilities than their Division II and III counterparts.
- Division II: Emphasizing a balance between athletics, academics, and extracurricular engagement, Division II institutions are required to sponsor at least five sports for men and five for women. Scholarships are available but are more limited than in Division I.
- Division III: Focusing primarily on the academic growth and personal development of student-athletes, Division III institutions do not offer athletic scholarships. Participation in sports is driven by the students' love for the game rather than scholarship incentives.

The governance of the NCAA is vested in committees that include representatives from member institutions. These committees are organized by divisions and cover various aspects of collegiate athletics, including rules compliance, academic standards, and championships.

NCAA Division I Athletic Departments: A Closer Look

NCAA Division I athletic departments represent the pinnacle of college sports, managing large-scale operations that integrate athletic success with academic achievement and community engagement. The structure and function of these departments are pivotal to sustaining the competitive edge and financial viability of their programs.

Leadership and Administration

The leadership and administration of an NCAA Division I athletic department are pivotal to its success, with the Athletic Director (AD) serving as the cornerstone of this complex structure. As the chief architect of the department's strategic direction, the AD oversees a broad range of functions, from compliance and academic services to operations, marketing, and finance. The scope of responsibilities and the challenges faced by an AD at the Division I level are significantly more complex and demanding than those at lower division levels.

At the Division I level, the role of the AD transcends mere administration. They are the face of the department, responsible for fostering an environment that balances athletic excellence with academic integrity and community engagement. Their leadership style and decisions have far-reaching implications for the department's reputation, financial health, and competitive success. Key responsibilities include:

- Strategic Planning and Policy Development: The AD is responsible for setting the strategic direction of the athletic department, including long-term planning and policy development. They must ensure that the department's objectives align with the broader goals of the institution and comply with NCAA regulations.
- Budget Management and Financial Oversight: Managing an athletic department with budgets often in the tens or hundreds of millions of dollars requires a sophisticated understanding of finance. The AD oversees the allocation of resources across teams and departments, ensuring financial stability while pursuing opportunities for growth.
- Compliance and Risk Management: Ensuring adherence to NCAA regulations is critical to avoid sanctions that can tarnish the institution's reputation and impact its financial well-being. The AD must implement effective compliance and risk management strategies to mitigate potential violations.
- Athletic Performance and Student-Athlete Welfare: The AD plays a crucial role in supporting coaches and teams to achieve athletic success while ensuring the welfare of student-athletes. This includes advocating for facilities improvements, supporting health and wellness programs, and fostering an environment where athletes can excel both on and off the field.
- Fundraising and Development: Division I athletic departments rely heavily on donations, sponsorships, and revenue from high-profile sports. The AD is often at the forefront of fundraising efforts, engaging alumni, donors, and corporate sponsors to secure financial support for scholarships, facilities, and programmatic needs.
- Media Relations and Brand Management: As the spokesperson for

the athletic department, the AD manages relationships with the media and oversees marketing and branding efforts. They must effectively communicate the department's achievements and navigate crises to maintain a positive public image.

- Stakeholder Engagement: Building and maintaining relationships with key stakeholders, including faculty, alumni, students, and the local community, is a critical responsibility. The AD must ensure that the athletic department contributes positively to the campus culture and community spirit.
- Institutional Policy and Governance: The AD participates in institutional decision-making, representing the athletic department in discussions on policies and initiatives that impact the broader university community. Their input is essential in shaping policies that support the integration of athletics within the academic mission of the institution.

The role of a collegiate athletic director is multifaceted and demanding, requiring a unique blend of leadership, financial acumen, and a deep understanding of the collegiate athletic landscape. They must navigate the complexities of managing a high-profile athletic department while upholding the values of academic excellence and integrity. Much of the success of an NCAA Division I athletic department hinges on the AD's ability to lead with vision, manage resources effectively, and foster an environment that supports the holistic development of student-athletes.

Compliance

The Compliance Office is the linchpin in ensuring the integrity of an NCAA Division I athletic program, entrusted with interpreting and enforcing the complex set of rules laid out by the NCAA. Functioning as both a watchdog and an educational resource, the office's core aim is to align every departmental facet with NCAA regulations. Through active information dissemination and ongoing education about the ever-changing NCAA legislation, it strives to build a culture of awareness and ensures regulatory adherence at all levels of the department.

The Compliance Office spearheads efforts to proactively preempt violations by establishing a robust monitoring system that oversees recruiting activities, academic progression, and scholarship allocation. Additionally, it plays a crucial role in maintaining the amateurism of student-athletes, vigilantly overseeing any external engagements or financial benefits that could compromise their eligibility. This proactive monitoring and educational outreach are essential to preemptively identify and address any potential lapses or violations.

Working closely with national and conference offices to ensure transparency, the Compliance Office is vital in maintaining the institution's reputation and supporting the principles of fairness and equality intrinsic to collegiate sports. By championing compliance and ethical practices, the office not only shields the program from sanctions but also reinforces the values at the core of the NCAA's mission.

Academic Support Services

To ensure student-athletes thrive in the classroom and beyond, institutions implement comprehensive academic support services that are tailored to the unique challenges faced by those who balance competitive sport with rigorous academics. These services not only focus on meeting immediate educational needs through personalized tutoring and structured study halls but also provide long-term academic planning and career advising. By facilitating effective time management strategies, teaching study skills, and offering major and career exploration guidance, academic support services equip student-athletes with the tools necessary for academic achievement and personal development. Moreover, these services play a crucial role in guiding student-athletes towards graduation, thereby aligning athletic pursuits with the overarching goal of obtaining a degree and securing a successful future post-athletics.

Sports Medicine and Athletic Training

The sports medicine and athletic training departments within collegiate athletic departments are pivotal to the comprehensive health management of student-athletes. Staffed by certified and experienced professionals, these departments offer an integrative approach to healthcare that encompasses a wide spectrum of services crucial to athlete welfare. Athletic trainers, working in conjunction with sports medicine physicians, physiotherapists, and nutritionists, devise personalized injury prevention programs tailored to the physical demands of each sport. They utilize the latest research and technology in exercise physiology to enhance performance while minimizing the risk of injuries.

When injuries do occur, these specialized teams spring into action, providing immediate care that adheres to the highest medical standards. The continuum of care extends well beyond the initial treatment, involving meticulous rehabilitation protocols designed to restore athletes to full functionality. This comprehensive care model ensures that recovery is not just about returning to play, but about reconditioning athletes for peak performance with an eye toward long-term health and mobility. Additionally, these departments are often involved in educating athletes on proper nutrition, rest, and self-care techniques, contributing to a holistic approach to athlete health. By prioritizing the well-being of student-athletes, sports medicine and athletic training staffs affirm the institution's commitment to the physical and psychological health of its students, which is just as critical as their achievements in competition and academics.

Strength and Conditioning

In the realm of NCAA Division I athletics, strength and conditioning coaches are instrumental in elevating the performance of athletes to the highest echelons of collegiate sport. These specialized coaches possess a deep understanding of sports science and apply this knowledge to develop advanced physical training programs that are meticulously customized to the specific requirements of each sport and athlete. These programs are designed with a multifaceted approach to enhance core strength, explosive speed, enduring stamina, and dynamic agility— attributes that are essential for competitive excellence across all sports disciplines. By incorporating a variety of training methodologies, including weightlifting, plyometrics, aerobic conditioning, and flexibility exercises, strength and conditioning coaches work to fortify the athletic prowess of the student-athletes, thereby improving their competitive edge and reducing the risk of injury.

Facilities Management

The management of athletic facilities such as stadiums, arenas, practice fields, and training centers is critical to sustaining high-caliber athletic programs. Managers in charge of these facilities must balance a complex array of responsibilities, from ensuring the safety and security of the venues to optimizing their scheduling, maintenance, and operation. The role of facilities management extends beyond maintenance; it also includes ensuring compliance with legal standards such as the Americans with Disabilities Act (ADA), managing risks, and maintaining environmental sustainability.

New facility planning and management at this level demand a multi-faceted approach, including collaboration with architects and engineers, to create venues that meet both present needs and future demands. This involves innovative design for adaptability, considering growth patterns, and ensuring the facilities are not only functional but also foster a safe and positive environment for athletes and spectators. Facility managers must also consider the financial implications, ensuring projects are cost-effective, meet budget constraints, and address the ecological impact.

The role of facilities management in collegiate athletic departments is expansive, incorporating planning, development, and management to support quality athletic programs. With a focus on accessibility, safety, functionality, and aesthetics, these professionals contribute significantly to the overall experience of all stakeholders. As stewards of these athletic spaces, facility managers are tasked with the creation and maintenance of environments that are conducive to sporting excellence and fan engagement, while being responsive to the changing needs of the sports community and environmental standards.

Marketing and Communications

Collegiate athletic programs leverage marketing and communications efforts to enhance their visibility and brand, focusing on promoting games, engaging fans via social media, managing media relations, and developing merchandise and licensing agreements. Effective marketing not only boosts attendance and fan engagement but also generates significant revenue through ticket sales and sponsorships. Beyond just promoting game days, these strategies create narratives that embody the institution's spirit, its teams, and athletes, distributed across various media to resonate with fans and attract new followers. The crucial role of social media has emerged, enabling direct engagement with a tech-savvy fan base by sharing game highlights, behind-the-scenes content, and stories of perseverance and triumph, ensuring consistent messaging across digital and traditional media platforms.

The primary goal of marketing and communications in collegiate athletics is to support the program's financial sustainability and enhance its public image. Strategies to increase ticket sales include dynamic marketing campaigns and creating personalized fan experiences, such as meet-and-greets and fan appreciation events, which deepen fans' emotional connection to the teams. Merchandise and licensing agreements extend the brand's reach, while sponsorships are vital for revenue, with strategic communications demonstrating value to potential sponsors. These efforts collectively drive a program's success, ensuring it enjoys strong fan support and financial health.

Sports information plays a crucial role within college athletic departments, managing and disseminating athletic-related information to enhance visibility, engagement, and operational efficiency. This encompasses a wide range of activities, including publicizing game stats and player achievements, promoting events, and engaging with media and the public. By effectively communicating the narratives and successes of student-athletes and teams, sports information fosters community and institutional pride, serving as the primary liaison between the department and media. In the digital age, their responsibilities have expanded to digital media management, crucial for fan engagement, institutional loyalty, and recruitment, highlighting the operational importance of sports information in achieving the athletic department's goals of transparency, engagement, and strategic communication.

Fundraising and Development

Fundraising and development serve as crucial lifelines for collegiate athletic departments, acting as the bedrock of financial well-being and programmatic success. These endeavors extend beyond mere monetary accumulation; they are about building a community of invested stakeholders, whose patronage and support transcend fiscal contributions. Engaging alumni, nurturing donor relationships, and forging partnerships with corporate entities are strategic moves that foster long-term loyalty and financial backing. This community often feels a deep connection with the athletic programs, propelled by a shared history and a commitment to the institution's legacy.

The art of fundraising involves tailored campaigns that resonate with potential benefactors' values and interests, prompting them to invest in the future of student-athletes and the broader sports community. Development initiatives often spotlight the direct impact of contributions, from providing scholarships that open doors for deserving athletes to enhancing facilities that elevate the institution's competitive edge. These improvements not only benefit current team members but also serve as a draw for future talent, ensuring a cycle of excellence and growth.

Moreover, well-orchestrated development efforts underscore the narrative of sports as a unifying element within the educational journey, emphasizing the role athletics play in shaping leaders, building character, and enriching the student experience. Through galas, booster clubs, legacy programs, and targeted campaigns, athletic departments craft a compelling call to action that encourages a culture of giving. In turn, this philanthropy bolsters the department's capacity to meet emerging needs and embrace new opportunities, positioning the program to thrive amid an ever-evolving collegiate sports landscape.

Challenges and Opportunities

The operational landscape of NCAA athletic departments is a complex arena fraught with an ever-expanding financial "arms race." This fierce competition for resources was flagged as early as the 1991 Knight Foundation Commission report, which called for more robust presidential oversight to safeguard academic and fiscal integrity within collegiate athletics.

One of the core financial challenges stems from escalating revenues driven by lucrative television contracts and the creation of conference-specific networks, which have widened the fiscal gulf between the "power conferences" and the rest. In the 2015-2016 period, then-Power 5 conferences accrued a staggering $6 billion in revenue, dwarfing the combined earnings of other schools. This disparity creates a challenging environment for those institutions reliant on student fees and university subsidies, which struggle to remain competitive both athletically and financially.

This financial dichotomy does not just affect competition; it raises existential questions about the amateur status of college athletics. The debate on whether student-athletes who contribute significantly to these revenue streams should receive compensation is ongoing. Such discussions are indicative of the broader dialogue surrounding the commercialization of college sports and the responsibilities of institutions in managing their athletic department operations within an equitable and sustainable model.

The complexity of these issues presents NCAA Division I athletic departments with not only challenges but also opportunities to revisit their financial models, engage in more strategic planning, and advocate for a more equitable distribution of resources. There's an impetus to foster innovations that can bridge the financial chasm, such as developing alternative revenue streams, enhancing fan engagement, and building partnerships that extend beyond traditional revenue sources.

The need to balance fiscal sustainability with the provision of a high-quality collegiate athletic experience opens avenues for leadership in academic integration, athletic competitiveness, and community engagement. By focusing on the holistic development of student-athletes and fan-centric experiences, athletic departments can navigate these challenges to build resilient and thriving programs that align with the evolving ethos of intercollegiate athletics.

The NCAA, with its comprehensive structure and governance model, plays a crucial role in shaping the landscape of collegiate athletics in the United States. Division I athletic departments, in particular, operate as multifaceted organizations that not only strive for success in competition but also prioritize the academic achievement and overall well-being of their student-athletes. As the landscape of college sports continues to evolve, the organization of the NCAA and the operation of its member institutions' athletic departments will remain pivotal in navigating the complexities of intercollegiate athletics.

Discussion Questions

- Reflect on the impact of NCAA regulations and the divisional structure on the operations of an athletic department. How do these factors influence decision-making and strategic planning?
- Consider the role of the Compliance Office in maintaining the integrity of an NCAA program. What are the potential consequences of non-compliance for an athletic department?
- Discuss how academic support services and sports medicine contribute to the holistic development of student-athletes. How do these services align with the NCAA's mission?
- Explore the importance of facilities management and marketing in enhancing the collegiate athletic experience. What are the challenges faced in these areas, and how are they addressed?
- Evaluate the financial and operational challenges highlighted in the Knight Foundation Commission report. What strategies can athletic departments employ to address these challenges?
- Examine the opportunities for innovation within NCAA athletic departments to address the financial disparities between institutions. What are some alternative revenue streams?
- Discuss the balance between fiscal sustainability and providing a high-quality athletic experience. How can athletic departments achieve this balance?
- Envision the future of the NCAA's role in collegiate athletics as the landscape continues to evolve. What changes or adaptations might be necessary?

Case Study 5.1: NCAA Governance Restructuring

The NCAA (National Collegiate Athletic Association) is the governing body that oversees college athletics in the U.S. It is divided into three divisions with distinct competitive and financial environments. The organization's governance structure is primarily divided among committees composed of representatives from member institutions, all working together to ensure that intercollegiate athletics operate within the educational framework.

The Event
In response to escalating financial inequalities among conferences and institutions, the NCAA undertook a major restructuring of its governance model. This initiative was particularly focused on Division I, where the financial and competitive stakes are highest. A series of

incidents involving financial malfeasance and compliance violations sparked this move, culminating in the NCAA Division I Board of Directors, including a new subset of representatives from the Power 5 conferences, acquiring greater autonomy to enact policies specifically tailored to their needs.

The Impact
The restructured governance model provided more flexibility to the Power 5 conferences, sparking debate over the NCAA's ability to maintain a level playing field across all institutions. This led to questions about the relevance of the NCAA's overarching authority and the future of collegiate athletics. Critics argue that this move may exacerbate the divide between the "haves" and "have-nots," while proponents believe it allows for better management of the unique challenges faced by larger athletic programs.

Discussion
- How does the NCAA's restructuring of governance affect the balance of power among Division I institutions?
- What are the potential implications of giving more autonomy to the Power 5 conferences?
- How can smaller institutions remain competitive in an environment where larger conferences wield greater influence?
- What measures can the NCAA take to maintain a fair competitive landscape across all divisions?
- Discuss the role of financial considerations in the restructuring of NCAA governance. How does this affect the student-athlete experience?
- What could be the long-term effects of the governance restructuring on the NCAA's mission to integrate athletics into the educational experience of student-athletes?

Case 5.2: Knight Foundation Arms Race

The National Collegiate Athletic Association (NCAA) serves as the governing body for college sports in the United States, overseeing a vast network of institutions, conferences, and student-athletes. The organization ensures fair play, academic compliance, and the overall integrity of college athletics.

The Event
In recent years, the NCAA has witnessed an unprecedented financial "arms race," characterized by a wide fiscal gulf between power conferences and other schools. This was highlighted in a report by the Knight Foundation Commission which emphasized the need for

stronger presidential oversight within collegiate athletics. The Power 5 conferences generated $6 billion in revenue in the 2015-2016 period alone, underscoring the financial disparities and raising questions about the sustainability of college athletics' financial models.

The Impact

This disparity has not only affected athletic competition but also raised concerns about the amateur status of student-athletes and the ethics of commercialization in college sports. Institutions reliant on student fees and university subsidies find themselves in a challenging position to stay competitive. Moreover, the debate over whether student-athletes should receive compensation for their contributions to these revenue streams persists, reflecting broader concerns about equity and the commercial aspects of college sports.

Discussion

- How do the financial disparities between power conferences and other institutions affect the overall landscape of college athletics?
- What are the implications of the current financial model on the amateur status of student-athletes, and how might this influence future NCAA policies?
- In what ways can NCAA Division I athletic departments innovate to address the challenges presented by the financial "arms race"?
- Discuss the ethical considerations of commercialization in college sports and its impact on institutional responsibilities and student-athlete welfare.
- How can the NCAA and its member institutions work together to ensure a more equitable distribution of resources across all athletic programs?

Chapter 6
The Role of Conferences

Collegiate athletic conferences are critical to the management of intercollegiate athletics, significantly influencing the vision, direction, and operations of athletic departments. These conferences often reflect a shared organizational identity and philosophy among member institutions, which engage in both cooperation and competition within the conference framework. Their roles and responsibilities are vast, extending beyond the organization of athletic contests to encompass aspects like revenue distribution, academic integrity, eligibility compliance, and media relations.

Upon successful completion of this unit, students will be able to:

- Understand the organizational, managerial, and operational significance of conferences in the realm of intercollegiate athletics and articulate the various functions these conferences perform.
- Analyze the historical factors that have influenced the formation and affiliations of athletic conferences and evaluate how these factors continue to shape contemporary conference alignments and reconfigurations.
- Identify and explain the criteria for developing effective organizational goals within athletic conferences and discuss how such goals can enhance the performance of these entities.
- Explain the role of conferences in upholding the academic integrity and eligibility standards within intercollegiate athletics.
- Assess the impact of conference affiliation on a member institution's financial resources, athletic competitiveness, and academic standing.
- Explore and propose strategies for conferences to maintain relevance and effectiveness amidst changing landscapes in media rights, technology, and educational policies.

Defining Conferences and Their Importance

Conferences in collegiate athletics serve a multifaceted purpose, acting as a nexus for schools that share similar values and competitive scopes. As collective entities, they offer a blend of competition paired with cooperation, aligning institutions towards common goals while fostering an environment where athletic rivalry can thrive alongside academic excellence and student-athlete well-being. These voluntary associations are instrumental in organizing and streamlining the operations of collegiate sports, ensuring consistency and fairness in competition, and serving as a central figure in discussions surrounding policies and procedures within intercollegiate athletics.

At the heart of every conference is the principle of competitive balance – the idea that every institution within the conference has a fair chance to compete, thereby maintaining the integrity of the competition. This balance is achieved through the cooperative efforts of member institutions, which work together to ensure that competition remains keen yet equitable, with regulations that promote a level playing field for all participants. By doing so, conferences cultivate a dynamic where sportsmanship and rivalry coexist, enriching the collegiate athletic experience.

Conferences are more than just sporting affiliations; they are alliances that reflect the shared missions and strategic goals of their member institutions. This alignment transcends the boundaries of sports, embedding itself into the academic and administrative fabric of each member. Through unified objectives, conferences can advocate for collective interests, drive strategic planning, and implement policies that resonate with the core values of each institution.

The Origins and Evolution of Conferences

Examining the historical roots of conferences reveals their importance in shaping the regulatory landscape of collegiate athletics. The genesis of athletic conferences can be traced back to the late 19th and early 20th centuries, a time when intercollegiate athletics began to captivate the nation's interest. Initially, these gatherings of institutions were informal and sporadic, but the burgeoning popularity of college sports necessitated a more organized approach. Early conferences such as the Intercollegiate Conference of Faculty Representatives, now known as the Big Ten, were among the first to bring a semblance of order to the chaotic and rapidly growing field of collegiate sports.

These embryonic conferences quickly assumed a central role in policymaking, often exerting more influence than national bodies like the NCAA. They established eligibility rules, scheduled championships, and even set standards for amateurism that would shape the ethos of collegiate athletics. The policies crafted in the conference meeting rooms would eventually become the cornerstone of national regulations.

Conferences emerged as the answer to a pressing need for standardization across the increasingly competitive landscape. They introduced regulations that would address disparities in recruitment, scheduling, and financial investments, ensuring fairness and consistency in collegiate sports. Moreover, they became mediators, managing internal conflicts among member institutions and preserving the integrity of the games.

As collegiate athletics have evolved, so too have the conferences. The introduction of scholarships, the expansion of women's athletics, and the explosion of television rights have all required conferences to adapt and reformulate their roles. They have had to balance traditional values with commercial realities, academic priorities with athletic success, and local allegiances with national appeal.

Conferences have been instrumental in creating a controlled environment for intercollegiate sports to thrive. By enforcing rules and maintaining order, they have allowed for the sustainable growth of collegiate athletics. This has included the management of media rights, the establishment of postseason play, and the coordination with other governing bodies to ensure that student-athletes have a platform to excel both athletically and academically.

The Modern Conference

Today's collegiate athletic conferences carry the legacy of their historical origins into a modern era characterized by significant transformations in the realm of intercollegiate sports. Modern conferences must navigate a landscape marked by rapid technological advances, changing consumer behaviors, and significant economic pressures. hey must contend with issues such as conference realignment, media negotiations, and the impacts of technology on sports consumption. The evolution of conferences continues to reflect the changing landscape of collegiate athletics, requiring a balance between honoring tradition and embracing innovation.

Conference realignment has become a staple of modern collegiate athletics, prompted by the pursuit of increased revenues, expanded media markets, and strategic positioning within the national landscape. As traditional geographic boundaries become less relevant, conferences have sought to expand their footprint, often adding institutions with robust athletic programs and a large fanbase to bolster their competitive and commercial appeal.

Media negotiations have grown increasingly complex as conferences aim to maximize their exposure and revenue through broadcasting rights. The evolution of digital media platforms presents both an opportunity and a challenge, as conferences must devise strategies that cater to a fragmented audience while securing lucrative deals. The financial implications of these negotiations are profound, influencing everything from athlete recruitment to facility improvements.

The impact of technology on sports consumption cannot be underestimated. Conferences must adapt to changing viewing habits, such as the shift towards streaming services and on-demand content. This adaptation requires innovation in how sports are delivered and consumed, ensuring that fan engagement remains high even as traditional models of sports viewership evolve.

Conferences today must strike a delicate balance between preserving the tradition and embracing innovation. They are tasked with upholding the heritage and values that have been the bedrock of their existence while also implementing modern practices that respond to the evolving demands of stakeholders, including student-athletes, fans, and media partners.

The evolution of conferences continues unabated, with each passing year bringing new challenges and opportunities. As they look to the future, conferences must be agile, adapting their strategies to maintain relevance and competitiveness in an ever-changing environment. Whether it's through embracing new technologies, expanding their reach, or innovating their financial models, conferences must remain at the forefront of change to shape the future of collegiate athletics.

Modern conferences stand as guardians at the intersection of tradition and progress, steering their member institutions through the dynamic waters of contemporary sports. Their success hinges on the ability to effectively manage the complexities of today's athletic environment while fostering the growth and development of collegiate sports for tomorrow's generation. As they continue to evolve, conferences will undoubtedly play a pivotal role in defining the trajectory of intercollegiate athletics, preserving the essence of competition and community that has always been at their core.

Roles and Responsibilities of Conferences

Athletic conferences are critical to the collegiate sports landscape, blending competition with collaboration among member institutions to not only partake in sports but also to uphold educational and ethical standards. These conferences are key in setting and enforcing rules on student-athlete eligibility, maintaining academic integrity, and easing logistical challenges like team travel and game scheduling. Beyond logistics, they forge a shared identity, aligning schools with similar philosophies to ensure a consistent set of expectations in sports and education. Essentially, conferences safeguard the collegiate athletic ethos, harmonizing excellence in sports with the academic and social values of their institutions.

Structuring Competition and Collaboration

Conferences structure intercollegiate athletics competitions, creating schedules that balance athletic demands with academic priorities. As entities within the NCAA structure, Division I conferences, for example, must comprise at least seven member institutions and offer a minimum of 12 sports, ensuring inclusivity of both men's and women's basketball. They provide a platform for collaborative efforts, enabling institutions to share insights and enhance their educational and athletic programs. Moreover, conferences assume legislative power, guiding championship events and setting forth rules—often more stringent than the NCAA's— to uphold high standards, as exemplified by the Ivy League's stance on athletic scholarships.

Conferences are also the nexus for championships in sports supported by the member institutions, establishing competition guidelines through collective decision-making. Financially, they can be significant, with revenue-sharing programs redistributing earnings from various sources, including NCAA distributions, TV contracts, and football bowl games, among members. This financial collaboration, bolstered by the emergence of conference-owned television networks like the SEC Network, can yield substantial payouts for member schools, illustrating the lucrative aspect of conference affiliation. Moreover, the dynamics of conference realignment, driven by factors such as television exposure and increased revenue potential, continually shape the college athletics landscape, reflecting the evolving priorities and strategic positioning of institutions within the sports sector.

Managing Revenue and Resources

Conferences in intercollegiate athletics play a pivotal role in managing both the revenue streams and the allocation of resources across their member institutions. The management of such revenue is crucial, as it directly supports athletic programs, contributing to their sustainability and competitiveness. Generated from various sources such as media rights, sponsorships, and athletic events, this revenue is strategically distributed to balance athletic needs with academic integrity. Conferences, thus, operate under a shared financial responsibility model, ensuring that each member institution benefits from the collective bargaining power and marketing efforts that would be far less impactful if done individually.

Furthermore, conferences are tasked with the equitable distribution of resources to foster fair competition and support the holistic development of student-athletes. This involves ensuring that facilities, training programs, and educational support services are funded adequately. By doing so, conferences not only uphold the sportsmanship and integrity of the games but also contribute to the academic and personal growth of the athletes. Such a role is complex, requiring constant adaptation to changing landscapes, such as fluctuating market values of media rights, sponsorship sensitivities, and the evolution of digital platforms affecting sports consumption. Conferences, hence, must remain agile and visionary, continually reassessing their strategies to optimize revenue and resource management, supporting their institutions' quest for excellence both in the arena and in the classroom.

Upholding Academic Integrity

A critical role of conferences is to uphold the academic integrity of their member institutions, maintaining the delicate balance between athletic aspirations and educational achievements. The foundation for this oversight can be traced back to early collaborations among educational institutions. For instance, the 1895 "Chicago Conference," attended by faculty representatives who would later establish the Big Ten Conference, marked a successful early effort to control and regulate the eligibility of student-athletes. This gathering was instrumental in formulating an approach to dealing with academic issues, paving the way for conferences to play a substantial role in the academic oversight of student-athletes.

Today's conferences, especially the major "power" conferences, are increasingly influential due to lucrative media deals and are central to the debate over collegiate athletics, particularly in the Football Bowl Subdivision (FBS) football. The growth in power and influence of these conferences presents challenges to the NCAA's governance and raises important questions for the future of college athletics. Conferences ensure that student-athletes meet the academic standards set by governing bodies, emphasizing the principle that participation in athletics should enhance, not hinder, the educational experience. This ongoing commitment to academic excellence is a cornerstone of their mission, demonstrating that conferences are not merely about sports but are also deeply invested in the educational welfare of the athletes.

Compliance and Eligibility

Conferences are pivotal in assuring that the intercollegiate athletic environment operates within the bounds of compliance and academic integrity. By enforcing regulations set forth by the NCAA and other governing bodies, conferences ensure that all athletes meet eligibility requirements, thus maintaining the integrity of collegiate sports. This duty involves meticulous verification of academic performance, athletic eligibility, and adherence to rules concerning recruitment and financial aid. The Academic Progress Rate (APR) and Graduation Success Rate (GSR) are instrumental metrics in this regard. The APR provides a real-time look at a team's academic success each semester by tracking the academic progress of each student-athlete on scholarship, accounting for eligibility, retention, and graduation. The GSR, on the other hand, offers a more comprehensive long-term view of student-athlete graduation success by considering the proportion of athletes who graduate within a given timeframe.

The responsibilities of conferences extend beyond mere regulation to ensuring a nurturing environment for student-athletes that encourages both athletic and academic excellence. In essence, conferences serve as custodians of educational values within the athletic sphere. They adopt a holistic approach, ensuring that institutions provide proper academic support, including tutoring, study halls, and life skills programs, all designed to foster student-athletes' growth. This integrated focus helps student-athletes to not only excel on the field but also to achieve significant academic milestones, preparing them for success beyond their collegiate sports careers. Through such concerted efforts, conferences reinforce the idea that while athletic prowess may be temporary, educational attainment lasts a lifetime.

Media and Public Relations

Conferences in collegiate athletics have a pivotal role in shaping the public perception and representation of their member institutions and sports programs. They are tasked with navigating complex media landscapes to secure media rights, which directly influence the visibility and commercial value of collegiate sports. In this dynamic field, conferences negotiate lucrative contracts that dictate how events are broadcasted, ensuring maximum exposure and revenue generation. Furthermore, conferences take on the crucial responsibility of managing public relations. Their efforts aim to cultivate and maintain a positive public image for their member institutions and their athletic programs, highlighting accomplishments and advocating for their value within both the educational system and the broader community. They serve as the communicators and promoters, continually engaging with various stakeholders from students, faculty, and alumni to the wider public, media, and businesses. Through strategic communication, they enhance public understanding, correct misconceptions, and address challenges, ultimately fostering a favorable environment for physical education and sports programs.

Public relations within collegiate sports conferences are multifaceted, involving a blend of promotion, education, and crisis management. By serving as a positive public information source, conferences elevate awareness about school activities, accomplishments, and participant successes. They work to build confidence in school systems and gather support for organizational funding and programs, all while stressing the value of education for all individuals. A conference's PR strategy seeks to improve communication and understanding among all community members, and actively establishes communication channels with media outlets. This approach is crucial in correcting misunderstandings and misinformation, including managing crises, concerning the mission and objectives of member schools, their programs, and organizations. By shaping a healthy public image for sports, they enable public relations personnel to maintain and sustain their programs effectively, identifying new marketing opportunities, and addressing community needs through the delivery of quality sports and educational programs.

Advantages of Conference Membership

Conferences in collegiate athletics offer a multitude of benefits and advantages to their member institutions, effectively serving as "orbits of competition" that foster a healthy balance between cooperation and competition. These alliances are formed on the basis of mutual respect, comparable academic standards, and a shared vision for the role of athletics within educational frameworks. The very essence of these competitive orbits lies in the harmonious coexistence of cooperation and competition, where member schools come together to share resources and strategies for mutual betterment, yet vigorously compete in various arenas including sports victories, media attention, recruitment, and financial resources. This competition can also become a potential source of conflict, necessitating a trust-based environment where institutions work towards common goals while maintaining their individual integrity. The commonalities shared among institutions within a conference not only drive competition in athletics but also extend into other domains such as student recruitment, faculty retention, and research funding. This broader competitive spectrum elevates the standards and expectations within the conference, encouraging member schools to continually benchmark their performance across all facets of their operation. Each victory within a conference, whether on the field or off, thus becomes a reflection of the combined efforts and shared objectives of its members, making the conference a vital measuring stick of success.

Conferences have also evolved over time, adapting to the changing dynamics of intercollegiate athletics. Historical expansions, such as the growth of the Pac-8 to the Pac-12, illustrate the fluid nature of conference affiliations and the strategic considerations that drive them, including geographic proximity, institutional compatibility, and shared goals. The formation and development of conferences are guided by SMART goals, which encapsulate specificity, meaningfulness, acceptance by participants, realistic yet challenging nature, and a clear time frame. These principles ensure that conferences remain focused, motivated, inclusive, ambitious, and timely in their actions and policies, continuously evolving to meet the needs of their members and the broader intercollegiate athletic environment.

Recent shifts in conference alignment, spurred by a desire to maximize financial gains through media rights and to remain competitive at the national level, have led to significant changes in NCAA Division I affiliations. These realignments are often goal-driven, aiming to meet NCAA bylaws for hosting championship games and securing broadcast agreements, reflecting a strategic approach to conference growth and sustainability. Benchmarking against the best-managed organizations, including other conferences, is an integral part of this strategic growth, as it provides role models for successful governance and performance metrics, as evidenced in the post-season evaluations and adjustments made by conferences like the Big 12.

The Future of Conferences

The future of intercollegiate athletic conferences is indeed a dynamic narrative, shaping the course of college sports and institutions involved. The benefits of conference membership will increasingly hinge on how these entities adapt to the shifting terrain of media rights, public expectations, and evolving educational paradigms.

One significant trend that has emerged in the 21st century is the realignment of conference affiliations, particularly within NCAA Division I, where traditional geographies and alliances have been reshaped by strategic moves aimed at maximizing television revenue, expanding market reach, and aligning with institutions of similar stature and aspiration. Such realignments often reflect an institution's ambition to enhance its competitive stance and financial position within the intercollegiate athletics ecosystem.

With the evolving media landscape, where digital platforms are gaining on traditional broadcast outlets, conferences must be astute in leveraging these new mediums to enhance visibility and revenue streams. This adaptation is not merely about broadcasting games but extends into creating content that engages fans year-round, expanding the reach and influence of conference brands.

Concurrently, public expectations around collegiate athletics are also transforming. There is a growing focus on athlete welfare, including their educational opportunities and life beyond sports. Conferences must, therefore, foster environments where athletic endeavors do not come at the expense of academic progress, aligning with broader institutional goals of educational excellence.

Educational standards and the balancing act between athletics and academics will remain a central concern for conferences. As the debate over the role and compensation of student-athletes continues, conferences will play a pivotal role in navigating these complex issues, advocating for policies and practices that uphold the integrity of both the sport and the education system.

Looking to the future, conferences will need to innovate not only to stay relevant but to actively shape the narrative of what intercollegiate athletics should represent. This may include exploring new markets, investing in technologies that enhance fan experience, and ensuring that the welfare and development of student-athletes remain central to their missions.

In essence, the future of conferences lies in their ability to be nimble, forward-thinking, and inclusive of the various stakeholders within the intercollegiate athletic community. By doing so, they can ensure that their membership continues to benefit from the rich tradition of competitive sports, while also adapting to the ever-changing landscape of higher education and athletics.

NCAA FBS Conferences

American Athletic Conference (AAC)

Army Black Knights
Charlotte 49ers
East Carolina Pirates
Florida Atlantic Owls
Memphis Tigers
Navy Midshipmen
North Texas Mean Green
Rice Owls
South Florida Bulls
Temple Owls
Tulane Green Wave
Tulsa Golden Hurricane
UAB Blazers
UTSA Roadrunners

Atlantic Coast Conference (ACC)

Boston College Eagles
California Golden Bears
Clemson Tigers
Duke Blue Devils
Florida State Seminoles
Georgia Tech Yellowjackets
Louisville Cardinals
Miami (FL) Hurricanes
North Carolina State Wolfpack
North Carolina Tar Heels
Pittsburgh Panthers
SMU Mustangs
Stanford Cardinal
Syracuse Orange
Virginia Cavaliers
Virginia Tech Hokies
Wake Forest Demib Deacons

Big Ten Conference

Illinois Fighting Illini
Indiana Hoosiers
Iowa Hawkeyes
Maryland Terrapins
Michigan Wolverines
Michigan State Spartans
Minnesota Golden Gophers

Nebraska Cornhuskers
Northwestern Wildcats
Ohio State Buckeyes
Oregon Ducks
Penn State Nittany Lions
Purdue Boilermakers
Rutgers Scarlet Knights
UCLA Bruins
USC Trojans
Washington Huskies
Wisconsin Badgers

Big 12 Conference
Arizona Wildcats
Arizona State Sun Devils
Baylor Bears
BYU Cougars
Cincinnati Bearcats
Colorado Buffaloes
Houston Cougars
Iowa State Cyclones
Kansas Jayhawks
Kansas State Wildcats
Oklahoma State Cowboys
TCU Horned Frogs
Texas Tech Red Raiders
UCF Knights
Utah Utes
West Virginia Mountaineers

Conference USA (CUSA)
FIU Panthers
Jacksonville State Gamecocks
Kennesaw State Owls
Liberty Flames
Louisiana Tech Bulldogs
Middle Tennessee Blue Raiders
New Mexico State Aggies
Sam Houston Bearkats
UTEP Miners
Western Kentucky Hilltoppers

Mid-American Conference (MAC)
Akron Zips
Ball State Cardinals

Bowling Green Falcons
Buffalo Bulls
Central Michigan Chippewas
Eastern Michigan Eagles
Kent State Golden Flashes
Miami (OH) RedHawks
Northern Illinois Huskies
Ohio Bobcats
Toledo Rockets
Western Michigan Broncos

Mountain West Conference
Air Force Falcons
Boise State Broncos
Colorado State Rams
Fresno State Bulldogs
Hawaii Rainbow Warriors
Nevada Wolfpack
New Mexico Lobos
San Diego State Aztecs
San Jose State Spartans
UNLV Rebels
Utah State Aggies
Wyoming Cowboys

Pac-12 Conference
Oregon State Beavers
Washington State Cougars

The departure of USC and UCLA catalyzed a major shakeup in the Pac-12 Conference, resulting in nearly all teams leaving due to media rights uncertainties, effectively dismantling the conference. This shift significantly affects the 2024 college football season's bowl game affiliations, with the 10 exiting teams still tied to the Pac-12's bowl agreements, except for the College Football Playoff games. Currently committed to bowls like the Alamo, Holiday, Las Vegas, Sun, LA, and Independence Bowls, the Pac-12, now down to two teams, cannot meet these commitments. However, with the contracts set to last two more seasons, it's expected that the departing teams will fulfill their bowl game obligations until these agreements expire. The majority of Oregon State's and Washington State's schedules will be comprised of Mountain West schools, although games against Oregon State and Washington State will not count toward the Mountain West Conference standings, nor will these two schools be eligible to participate in the Mountain West Conference Championship game.

Southeastern Conference (SEC)
Alabama Crimson Tide
Arkansas Razorbacks
Auburn Tigers
Florida Gators
Georgia Bulldogs
Kentucky Wildcats
LSU Tigers
Mississippi State Bulldogs
Missouri Tigers
Oklahoma Sooners
Ole Miss Rebels
South Carolina Gamecocks
Tennessee Volunteers
Texas Longhorns
Texas A&M Aggies
Vanderbilt Commodores

Sun Belt Conference
Appalachian State Mountaineers
Coastal Carolina Chanticleers
Georgia Southern Eagles
Georgia State Panthers
James Madison Dukes
Marshall Thundering Herd
Old Dominion Monarchs
Arkansas State Red Wolves
Louisiana Ragin' Cajuns
Louisiana-Monroe Warhawks
South Alabama Jaguars
Southern Miss Golden Eagles
Texas State Bobcats
Troy Trojans

FBS Independents
Notre Dame Fighting Irish
UConn Huskies
UMass Minutemen

FBS independents in college football opt out of conference affiliation for strategic, historical, and financial reasons, such as scheduling flexibility, preservation of traditional rivalries, and the negotiation of lucrative broadcasting deals. Notre Dame's independence, underpinned by advantages like control over scheduling and a profitable NBC deal, enhances its national brand and recruiting reach while preserving its historic rivalries and traditions. UConn's move to independence in 2020, prompted by conference realignment challenges, allowed for more flexible game scheduling and a focus on rebuilding, alongside aligning its other sports with traditional Big East rivals. Despite the advantages of autonomy and potential for increased revenue and national exposure, challenges remain, including difficult scheduling and securing paths to major bowl games or the College Football Playoff (CFP). Nonetheless, independent teams are eligible for postseason bowls and the CFP, with their performance, strength of schedule, and notable wins being critical for selection, thereby ensuring that high-performing independents have a pathway to compete for the national championship.

Discussion Questions

- How do conferences navigate the balance between enhancing competition and maintaining academic integrity?
- What are the most significant ways that conferences contribute to the financial stability of their member institutions?
- In what ways do conferences advocate for the interests of their members, and how does this impact national discussions in collegiate sports?
- Discuss the challenges and opportunities that arise from conference realignments. What are the motivations behind these strategic moves?
- How have digital media platforms changed the way conferences manage their media rights and public relations?
- Reflect on the role of conferences in upholding academic standards. How does this affect the daily lives of student-athletes?

Case Study 6.1: Conference Realignment

Conference realignment refers to the process by which collegiate athletic programs switch their association from one conference to another. This phenomenon has become increasingly common in the landscape of college athletics, driven by a complex interplay of financial incentives, competitive aspirations, media rights, and geographic considerations. Historically, athletic conferences were formed based on geographic proximity and academic affiliations, but recent decades have seen a shift towards realignments that prioritize television revenue, market expansion, and strategic positioning within the national landscape of collegiate sports.

The Event
The trend of conference realignment gained significant momentum in the early 21st century, marked by high-profile moves that reshaped the

traditional boundaries and affiliations of college sports conferences. These realignments often involve schools from major conferences seeking to enhance their competitive stance, financial position, and national visibility. A notable example is the realignment that saw universities traditionally associated with one geographic region or conference moving to another for perceived benefits, such as increased television revenue, access to larger markets, and improved competitive opportunities.

The Impact
- Financial Implications: Schools moving to more lucrative conferences can significantly increase their revenue from television contracts and media rights, which in turn can be invested in improving athletic facilities, recruiting, and overall program competitiveness.
- Competitive Balance: Realignment can disrupt the traditional competitive balance within conferences, as powerhouse programs may join weaker conferences and dominate, or alternatively, find themselves challenged more consistently in a stronger conference.
- Fan and Rivalry Dynamics: Traditional rivalries may be disrupted or ended, affecting fan engagement and diminishing the cultural and historical ties that contribute to the college sports experience.
- Geographic Considerations: The geographic coherence of conferences can be diluted, leading to increased travel costs and time, impacting student-athlete welfare and academic responsibilities.

Discussion
- What are the primary drivers behind conference realignment, and how do they reflect the evolving priorities of collegiate athletic programs?
- In what ways can conference realignment impact the student-athlete experience, both positively and negatively?
- How do fans and alumni perceive conference realignment, especially when traditional rivalries are disrupted or discontinued?
- What strategies can conferences employ to mitigate the potential negative effects of realignment on competitive balance, geographic coherence, and student-athlete welfare?

Case Study 6.2: The Dissolution of a Major Athletic Conference

The dissolution of a major athletic conference, such as the Pac-12, represents a significant shift in the landscape of collegiate athletics. The Pac-12, known for its rich history, competitive excellence, and academic prestige, comprises universities across the western United States. A dissolution scenario would likely stem from complex factors, including financial pressures, conference realignment, competitive imbalances, and evolving media rights landscapes.

The Event

The dissolution of an entire conference is precipitated by a combination of unsustainable financial models, disagreements among member institutions on strategic directions, and the lure of more lucrative media rights deals from other conferences. Several key members initiate departure negotiations with other conferences, seeking improved financial stability, enhanced competitive opportunities, and better alignment with their strategic goals. As these departures destabilize the conference, remaining members are forced to consider their options, leading to a chain reaction that culminates in the dissolution of the conference.

The Impact

- Member Institutions: Universities face the challenge of securing new conference affiliations, which may significantly impact their athletic programs' financial health, competitive dynamics, and traditional rivalries.
- Athletes and Recruiting: Student-athletes experience uncertainty regarding their competitive futures, and recruiting dynamics shift as institutions navigate the transition to new conferences.
- Financial Ramifications: The dissolution disrupts existing media rights agreements, sponsorship deals, and revenue-sharing, requiring extensive negotiations to secure new financial arrangements.
- Fan and Alumni Engagement: Fans and alumni may feel alienated or disheartened by the loss of traditional rivalries and the historic identity associated with the conference, potentially impacting long-term support and engagement.

Discussion

- What strategies can institutions employ to navigate the financial and competitive challenges posed by the dissolution of a major conference?
- How can conferences and institutions work to preserve student-athlete welfare and academic integrity during periods of significant athletic realignment?
- In what ways can new media rights agreements be structured to promote long-term stability and growth for collegiate athletic programs post-dissolution?
- How can institutions maintain or rekindle fan and alumni engagement amidst the upheaval of traditional conference affiliations and rivalries?
- What lessons can be learned from the dissolution of a major conference in terms of governance, financial management, and strategic planning within collegiate athletics?

Chapter 7
Goals and Mission Statements

In the dynamic landscape of intercollegiate athletics, the articulation of clear goals and the crafting of effective mission statements serve as the compass that guides athletic departments toward success. This chapter delves into the paramount importance of departmental goals and the art of formulating impactful mission statements. We will explore how these tools not only define the identity and direction of athletic programs but also reflect their values, aspirations, and commitment to both excellence and integrity.

Upon successful completion of this unit, students will be able to:

- Understand the importance of clear, well-defined goals and mission statements in intercollegiate athletic departments.
- Articulate the process of aligning departmental goals and mission statements with the broader values and objectives of the academic institution.
- Identify the critical components of effective mission statements and how they communicate the department's purpose, values, and commitments to various stakeholders.
- Engage stakeholders in the development of goals and mission statements.
- Navigate and address the challenges associated with balancing competitive success, academic integrity, and resource management in the establishment of goals and mission statements.
- Apply principles learned to analyze and critique existing goals and mission statements of intercollegiate athletic departments.

The Role of Goals in Athletic Departments

Goals in an athletic department are a multifaceted construct central to the planning, execution, and evaluation of a department's initiatives and strategies. As benchmarks for success, these goals provide the clarity and direction necessary for an athletic department to function optimally. By setting objectives such as enhancing the welfare of student-athletes, achieving competitive success, ensuring academic excellence, and promoting diversity and inclusion, an athletic department lays out a roadmap for its journey towards excellence. These goals are more than mere checkpoints; they encapsulate the department's vision and operational priorities, making it possible to allocate resources efficiently, make decisions that are informed by clear targets, and methodically measure progress against established standards.

The prioritization of resources is perhaps one of the most tangible benefits of well-defined goals. In an environment where financial, human, and physical resources are often limited, clear goals enable managers to allocate these assets judiciously. Decisions about where to invest become easier and more strategic when there are clear objectives to meet. For instance, a goal focused on enhancing student-athlete welfare might lead to investment in mental health resources, while a goal aimed at competitive success might prioritize state-of-the-art training facilities. This strategic allocation of resources, guided by concrete goals, ensures that every decision is a stepping stone toward the desired outcomes for the department.

On a more intangible level, goals engender a sense of purpose and motivation across the board, from administrative staff to the athletes themselves. When individuals understand how their daily efforts contribute to larger ambitions, their work gains meaning and urgency. Goals unite teams, fostering a culture of collaboration and shared commitment. They help in transforming individual accomplishments into collective victories, aligning the diverse efforts of various stakeholders with the department's overarching ambitions. As members of the department, from coaches to support staff, strive towards a common set of goals, they forge a powerful synergy that propels the department forward, not just in terms of athletic performance but as a leader in holistic student-athlete development.

Crafting Effective Mission Statements

A mission statement, on the other hand, is a concise declaration of the department's core purpose, essentially answering the question, "Why do we exist?" It captures the essence of an athletic department's goals, values, and ethos, serving as a public declaration of its commitment to stakeholders, including student-athletes, the academic institution, alumni, and the community at large. A well-crafted mission statement not only guides decision-making and strategy but also communicates to the outside world what the department stands for.

Crafting an effective mission statement is an exercise in reflection and precision for an athletic department. It is a process of distilling the department's identity, values, and purpose into a clear and compelling narrative. A well-articulated mission statement acts as a beacon that illuminates the department's path, serving not only as a foundational reference for decision-making but also as a unifying declaration for all associated parties. It encapsulates the broader intentions of the athletic department, going beyond mere objectives to address the ethical and philosophical underpinnings of its existence. As such, the mission statement serves as a touchstone for the department's various endeavors, ensuring that all initiatives are aligned with the central tenets of the institution's athletic philosophy.

The creation of a mission statement goes beyond summarizing current practices; it involves a visionary outlook that projects the department's long-term aspirations. This narrative should be inspirational yet achievable, resonating with a wide audience, from student-athletes who live the mission daily to alumni and donors who support it. A mission statement must articulate a compelling vision that can rally support and drive collective action. It must be crafted thoughtfully to ensure it is broad enough to encompass the full range of athletic department activities while specific enough to provide clear direction. Through the mission statement, the department communicates its dedication to fostering an environment that nurtures athletic excellence, academic integrity, and personal growth.

Finally, an effective mission statement must be communicated and integrated into the very fabric of the department's culture. It is not a mere slogan to be recited but a set of principles to be embodied in the actions and decisions of all stakeholders. It should be evident in the daily operations of the department, from recruitment and coaching practices to community engagement and alumni relations. By living out its mission statement, the department solidifies its identity and builds a strong, cohesive brand that is recognized and respected both within and outside the institution. The mission statement thus becomes a living document, dynamically shaping and being shaped by the evolving landscape of intercollegiate athletics and the department's response to it.

Aligning Goals with Institutional Values

Aligning the goals of an athletic department with the broader values and objectives of its parent academic institution is a strategic imperative that underlies the department's ability to succeed and contribute meaningfully to the university's overarching mission. This synchronization ensures that the athletic programs amplify the institution's reputation, drawing on shared principles and aspirations to create a powerful synergy between academic and athletic excellence. Effective alignment requires an intimate understanding of the university's core academic mission, its commitment to social responsibility, and the ethical standards it upholds. Athletic department goals that resonate with these institutional values not only validate the role of athletics within the university context but also strengthen the institution's identity and brand, fostering a sense of unity and shared purpose across the entire university community.

Embedding an institution's values into the operations and culture of its athletic department is a process that demands active engagement and thoughtful implementation. It is not enough for the athletic department to acknowledge these values in theory; they must be woven into the fabric of the department's daily practices. This includes recruitment strategies that prioritize academic achievement, community service initiatives that reflect social commitments, and governance practices that uphold the highest ethical standards. By infusing the institution's values into every aspect of their operations, athletic departments can create an environment that is conducive to the development of student-athletes who are not only champions in their sports but also ambassadors of the university's values and contributors to its mission.

Engaging Stakeholders in Goal Setting

Engaging stakeholders in the goal-setting process is a fundamental aspect of creating a robust and inclusive athletic department. When stakeholders such as student-athletes, coaches, administrative staff, faculty, alumni, and the community are invited to contribute to discussions regarding the department's direction and priorities, it ensures a multi-faceted perspective that enriches the decision-making process.

Such inclusion cultivates a broad-based investment in the department's future, with each group bringing unique insights and concerns to the table. By acknowledging and valuing the voice of each stakeholder, the athletic department not only garners a wealth of ideas and experiences but also engenders a collective spirit and shared ownership over the goals set. This collaborative approach is crucial for fostering a sense of belonging and for driving concerted efforts towards common objectives.

Moreover, involving stakeholders in the conception and implementation of goals does more than just diversify input; it solidifies trust and promotes an environment of transparency. As stakeholders see their input taken seriously and their concerns addressed, they are more likely to support the athletic department's initiatives and advocate for its success. This engagement also fortifies the relationship between the department and its wider community, forging bonds that are critical during times of celebration and challenge alike. In a larger sense, the integration of diverse stakeholder viewpoints helps to construct an athletic department that is reflective of and responsive to the community it serves, thereby strengthening its foundation and facilitating the achievement of shared aspirations.

Balancing Competitive Success and Academic Excellence

In the realm of intercollegiate athletics, where the glint of trophies and the roar of the crowd can overshadow the silent but significant accomplishments in the classroom, striking a balance between competitive success and academic excellence is essential. Goals and mission statements of an athletic department must navigate this delicate equilibrium, reinforcing the commitment to develop student-athletes who excel in both arenas. This balance is a commitment to nurturing well-rounded individuals for whom athletic prowess is matched by intellectual rigor. By setting goals that value academic achievements as highly as athletic ones, a department pledges to support its student-athletes in classrooms and in competition alike, recognizing that the true measure of success extends beyond the playing field. These goals should serve as a reminder that the department is dedicated to equipping student-athletes with the skills, knowledge, and critical thinking abilities necessary for life after sports.

Mission statements should echo this commitment, embodying the department's holistic view of student development. They should articulate a vision of athletic programs that function synergistically with educational objectives, rather than in competition with them. Emphasizing the importance of personal growth and the acquisition of life skills positions the athletic department as an integral player in the educational mission of the institution. This dual focus on competitive success and academic excellence requires the development of support structures and resources tailored to the needs of student-athletes, ensuring that the athletic department's objectives are actionable and accountable. Ultimately, goals and mission statements crafted with this balance in mind will cultivate an environment where student-athletes are encouraged to aspire to excellence in all facets of their lives, with the department's support every step of the way.

Adapting to Change and Managing Resources

The landscape of intercollegiate athletics is in a constant state of flux, with evolving regulations, fluctuating levels of competition, and changing societal values. For athletic departments, the capacity to adapt is crucial. Goals and mission statements are not set in stone; they must be living documents, able to evolve as the external environment demands. This agility ensures that departments stay aligned with the latest NCAA regulations, maintain competitiveness, and meet the changing expectations of athletes, students, and the community. Adapting goals and mission statements promptly and appropriately allows departments to navigate through the waters of change without losing sight of their core values and objectives. As external pressures and opportunities arise, athletic departments must reassess and recalibrate their strategic plans to remain effective and purpose-driven.

Resource management plays a critical role in the successful adaptation to change. An athletic department's goals are fundamentally tied to its resources—financial, human, and infrastructural. As objectives evolve, so too must the strategies for resource allocation. Athletic departments must be skilled in maximizing the use of their assets while also being realistic about their limitations. This requires a judicious balance between ambition and practicality. Efficient resource management means investing in areas that will yield the highest returns in terms of student-athlete development, competitive success, and institutional alignment. It also involves being proactive in seeking new resources and innovative in overcoming constraints, ensuring the sustainability and growth of athletic programs.

In an ever-evolving environment, the proactive management of change is indispensable. This goes beyond mere survival; it's about seizing the opportunity to lead and set new standards in intercollegiate athletics. Athletic departments that anticipate shifts, engage in strategic planning, and remain flexible in their approaches position themselves at the forefront of progress. By fostering a culture that is responsive to change, athletic departments can transform challenges into opportunities— adapting their mission to the zeitgeist, optimizing resource allocation, and achieving new heights of excellence. Whether navigating the complexities of student-athlete compensation, digital media rights, or emerging technologies, the ability to adapt is the bedrock of continued relevance and success in the competitive world of collegiate sports.

SMART Goals

SMART goals, a comprehensive framework for setting clear, achievable objectives, play a crucial role in both personal and professional development, including the realm of intercollegiate athletics administration. The acronym SMART encapsulates five critical criteria—Specific, Measurable, Achievable, Relevant, and Time-bound—each contributing to the creation of well-defined and trackable goals.

- Specific goals demand clarity and precision, compelling individuals to delineate their objectives explicitly. This specificity aids in focusing efforts and boosting motivation by answering essential questions about the goal's nature, importance, involved parties, location, and necessary resources or constraints.
- Measurable objectives allow for the tracking of progress, which is vital for maintaining motivation and focus. The ability to measure progress towards a goal ensures that individuals can assess their advancement, adjust their strategies as necessary, and experience the fulfillment that comes from getting closer to achieving their aspirations.
- Achievable goals are realistic and within one's grasp, yet they challenge abilities and encourage growth. Setting achievable goals involves recognizing and utilizing resources and opportunities that may have been previously overlooked, ensuring that the goals are ambitious yet attainable.
- Relevance ensures that the goal is significant and aligns with other pertinent objectives. It emphasizes the importance of setting goals that are not only beneficial for individual progress but also contribute to broader ambitions. Maintaining control over these goals is crucial, even when support and collaboration are necessary for achievement.
- Time-bound goals have explicit deadlines, providing a sense of urgency and a timeframe within which to strive for and achieve the set objectives. This aspect helps prioritize long-term goals over daily tasks, ensuring consistent progress towards the ultimate aim.

In the context of intercollegiate athletics administration, applying the SMART framework involves delineating both short-term and long-term objectives, which serve as a roadmap for future decisions and actions. Whether it's enhancing a professional network, completing coursework, or securing internships, SMART goals facilitate systematic planning and execution. They offer a structured approach to achieving personal ambitions, fostering leadership skills, and ensuring that each step taken is a stride towards realizing one's professional and academic aspirations. This meticulous planning not only fosters a sense of achievement but also cultivates effective leadership qualities essential for success in any field.

Lessons Learned and Best Practices

Academic institutions that have thrived in translating their athletic department's goals and mission statements into real-world success share a common practice: they ensure that these goals are intricately aligned with the larger values of the institution. Goals are set not only for competitive success but also for the development of student-athletes as well-rounded individuals. For example, a university might set a goal of achieving a certain win rate in competitions while simultaneously aiming for high academic performance among its athletes. This dual-focused goal-setting helps student-athletes to excel both on the field and in the classroom, and sets a precedent for the type of excellence the institution stands for. The key lesson here is the integration of athletics within the broader educational mission, which reinforces the message that academic institutions are places of learning first and foremost, with athletics serving as an extension of educational values.

Engagement with stakeholders is another cornerstone of best practices in this area. Institutions that stand out in terms of their athletic success and student welfare have engaged with not just athletes and coaches, but also with academic staff, alumni, and the local community in the goal-setting process. This participatory approach ensures that the goals and mission statements are reflective of the needs and ambitions of the entire university ecosystem. By taking into account the insights and aspirations of diverse stakeholders, these institutions can set goals that are ambitious yet achievable, and mission statements that resonate widely. These practices encourage the buy-in needed to pursue and achieve these goals collectively, thereby increasing the likelihood of success.

Finally, the most successful institutions demonstrate a capacity to balance diverse objectives within their athletic departments. They acknowledge that the pursuit of excellence in sports can be in tension with other objectives such as academic integrity, personal development, and community relations. To manage this, they set up frameworks that allow for the continuous evaluation and balancing of these sometimes competing interests. Furthermore, they remain adaptable to changes in the intercollegiate athletic landscape, such as shifts in regulations, societal expectations, and the advent of new technologies or practices. Institutions that can agilely navigate these changes are able to maintain their commitments to student-athlete welfare and community engagement, even as they pursue competitive greatness. The lesson here is that adaptability and the capacity to balance diverse objectives are critical to long-term success and positive reputation in the dynamic environment of collegiate athletics.

Goals and Mission Statements as Living Documents

Goals and mission statements are dynamic entities within athletic departments, serving not as fixed targets but as guiding north stars, adapting to the ebb and flow of an institution's life and the broader athletic field. Recognizing them as living documents emphasizes the need for regular reassessment, ensuring they remain relevant and reflective of an evolving set of priorities, both internally and in the broader context of intercollegiate athletics. The process of continuous evaluation is critical, especially as new challenges and opportunities arise, such as changes in student demographics, shifts in sports popularity, and updates in compliance regulations. Periodic review sessions that involve stakeholder feedback can lead to meaningful revisions that keep goals and mission statements fresh, ambitious, and aligned with the institution's current values and the latest trends in sports.

The process of updating these documents should be structured and strategic. It might involve annual reviews, or more frequent check-ins to discuss the developments within the department and the larger athletic arena. This process should be transparent and inclusive, involving coaches, athletes, administrative staff, alumni, and even fans. This breadth of perspective ensures a comprehensive understanding of the needs and opportunities faced by the department. Adjustments should be made with a clear understanding of the long-term vision of the department and should reflect a balance of aspirations and pragmatic considerations. The mission statement, particularly, should serve as a concise encapsulation of the department's enduring values, even as specific goals are tweaked to adapt to changing circumstances.

Effectively articulated goals and mission statements do more than guide the day-to-day operations of athletic departments; they lay the groundwork for a legacy of excellence and integrity. They are the pillars upon which athletic programs can build sustained success, not only in terms of wins and losses but in developing student-athletes who exemplify the highest standards of performance, sportsmanship, and community involvement. A well-crafted mission statement acts as a declaration of the department's commitment to these ideals, setting a clear direction for current initiatives and future endeavors. As such, the process of developing these statements should be thoughtful and deliberate, ensuring that they resonate with all members of the athletic community. This foundational work is crucial, as it does not just reflect the present ethos of the department but also ignites inspiration and commitment for future generations, leaving an indelible mark on the landscape of collegiate sports.

Discussion Questions

- How can an athletic department ensure that its goals and mission statements remain aligned with the dynamic values and objectives of the parent institution?
- What strategies can be used to engage various stakeholders in the goal-setting and mission-statement crafting process within an athletic department?
- Reflect on the balance between competitive success and academic excellence. How can athletic departments set goals that honor both, and why is this balance important?
- In what ways can goals and mission statements act as living documents that reflect the changing landscape of intercollegiate athletics? What are some best practices for their regular review and reassessment?
- How can mission statements and goals contribute to building a legacy of excellence and integrity in intercollegiate athletics? What are some examples of this in practice?
- What are the potential challenges of aligning an athletic department's mission and goals with the institution's values, and how can these challenges be addressed?
- How does the concept of mission statements and goals as living documents enhance the ability of an athletic department to adapt to the evolving demands of intercollegiate athletics?

Case Study 7.1: Goal Setting in a D-I Athletic Department

In the fiercely competitive realm of NCAA Division I athletics, a renowned public university recognized the need to redefine its athletic department's goals and mission statement. The department was historically successful but had recently encountered challenges with student-athlete academic performance and community engagement. The university prided itself on its storied athletic legacy and was committed to student-athlete welfare, academic excellence, and a strong community presence.

The Event
To address these issues, the department undertook a comprehensive goal-setting initiative. This process started with a series of workshops and consultations with all department stakeholders, including athletes, coaches, university administration, and alumni. The stakeholders identified key areas for improvement and innovation, such as academic support programs, athlete mental health, and engagement with the local community. As a result, the department set a clear and measurable goal to rank within the top 10 of the NCAA's Academic Progress Rate (APR)

within five years. Additionally, they aimed to enhance athlete well-being and community engagement through structured programs and partnerships.

The Impact

The newly set goals and revamped mission statement had a multifaceted impact. There was a noticeable increase in the academic performance of student-athletes, with the department achieving its APR goal in four years. The investment in mental health resources and community engagement initiatives also paid dividends, leading to improved athlete well-being and a stronger university-community relationship. The clear, strategic allocation of resources based on these goals resulted in better decision-making and more efficient use of the department's finances, human capital, and facilities. The department's mission statement, emphasizing the dual pursuit of academic and athletic excellence, became a rallying point for all involved.

Discussion

- How did involving various stakeholders in the goal-setting process contribute to the successful implementation of the new goals and mission statement?
- In what ways did the department's emphasis on academic achievement impact the culture within the athletic programs?
- How might the department measure the success of its community engagement initiatives?
- What challenges might the department face in maintaining its success in academic progress and community engagement, and how can it prepare to address these challenges?
- How can the department ensure that its goals and mission statement continue to evolve and remain relevant over time?

Case Study 7.2: Craft a Mission Statement for a Junior College

You are the new athletic director at a junior college that had long operated under a mission statement that was generic and failed to capture the unique spirit and challenges of their programs. The college prides itself on providing opportunities for student-athletes to excel both academically and athletically, serving as a stepping stone to four-year institutions. However, the existing mission statement did not reflect the department's commitment to these ideals, nor did it address the diverse backgrounds and needs of its student-athletes.

The Event

As the Athletic Director, you recognized the need for a mission statement that would encapsulate the department's core values and aspirations.

You initiated a comprehensive review process, involving stakeholders at all levels, from student-athletes and coaches to faculty and community members. This process was designed to glean insights into the collective vision for the department and to craft a statement that would guide the department's future endeavors. The result was a mission statement that spoke to the heart of the JC experience, emphasizing personal growth, academic success, athletic excellence, and a commitment to equity and community engagement.

The Impact

The new mission statement had a profound impact on the department. It provided a clear direction for policy decisions, the allocation of resources, and the development of athletic programs. The statement's emphasis on academic success led to the creation of enhanced academic support services for student-athletes. Its focus on equity resulted in proactive recruitment from underserved communities, broadening the diversity of the athletic program. The community engagement component led to increased partnerships with local organizations, enriching both the community and the student-athlete experience. Moreover, the mission statement became a rallying cry for the department, strengthening the identity and cohesion of the teams and enhancing the JC's reputation.

Discussion

- How can a mission statement influence the strategic direction and daily operations of a junior college athletic department?
- What are the potential challenges and benefits of engaging a diverse group of stakeholders in the crafting of a mission statement?
- In what ways can a mission statement contribute to the success and well-being of student-athletes at a junior college?
- How can an athletic department ensure that its mission statement remains relevant and reflective of its evolving priorities and the changing landscape of collegiate athletics?
- Discuss how a well-crafted mission statement can impact the legacy of a junior college athletic department and its student-athletes.

Chapter 8
Ethics in Collegiate Athletics

The realm of collegiate athletics occupies a unique and significant position within the broader landscape of higher education, intertwining the pursuit of academic excellence with the competitive spirit of sports. As such, it embodies a complex web of ethical considerations that span from fairness and integrity to inclusivity and student-athlete welfare. This chapter delves into the multifaceted ethical dimensions that govern collegiate athletics, examining how these principles influence policy-making, shape the behavior of key stakeholders, and impact the overall experience of student-athletes.

Upon successful completion of this unit, students will be able to:

- Understand the importance of ethical conduct in collegiate athletics.
- Assess the influence of reform efforts on collegiate athletics.
- Critically assess the effectiveness of these reforms and consider future directions for ethical improvement in collegiate sports.
- Apply ethical decision-making models to real-world scenarios in collegiate athletics.
- Develop strategies for fostering ethical leadership and accountability in collegiate athletics programs.
- Assess the mechanisms for ensuring accountability, including policy development, enforcement, and the cultivation of a culture that values ethical behavior and sportsmanship.

The Ethical Framework in Collegiate Athletics

At the heart of collegiate athletics lies a fundamental ethical framework designed to uphold the values of fairness, equity, and respect. This framework is not merely theoretical but is embedded in the policies and practices of institutions and governing bodies like the NCAA. It is a dynamic and comprehensive structure, rooted deeply in the tradition of upholding integrity in every aspect of sports. It represents a commitment to maintaining a level playing field where student-athletes can compete and grow, and it extends beyond the field or court, influencing the academic, personal, and social realms of a student-athlete's life.

Central to this ethical framework is the principle of gender equity, which is vital in ensuring that female athletes receive the same opportunities as their male counterparts. Title IX legislation was a significant leap forward in this regard, but its application goes beyond mere compliance. It inspires policies that promote equal access to training facilities, educational resources, and athletic scholarships. Furthermore, it requires institutions to support female sports programs actively, encouraging participation and fostering an environment where female athletes can excel and lead.

Sportsmanship, another pillar of this ethical framework, speaks to the heart of what it means to engage in collegiate athletics. It is the spirit of sportsmanship that compels athletes to perform with honor, to respect their opponents, and to accept outcomes with grace, regardless of the stakes. It's about fostering a sense of camaraderie and mutual respect among competitors, emphasizing the importance of the journey and the lessons learned, not just the final score. Institutions and coaches play a crucial role in instilling these values, teaching student-athletes that how they play the game is as important as winning.

The recruitment of student-athletes is also subject to ethical scrutiny. The process must be transparent, prioritizing the best interests of the prospective students. Recruiters and coaches hold the responsibility to accurately represent their programs, avoiding over-promising and ensuring that athletes are fully aware of what is expected of them both on and off the field. This extends to academic commitments, with institutions having an ethical obligation to support the educational pursuits of their athletes, ensuring that sports enhance rather than hinder their academic performance.

Lastly, the welfare of student-athletes is a comprehensive consideration that underpins the ethical framework. Institutions must safeguard the physical and mental health of athletes, provide adequate medical care, and ensure that athletes are not unduly pressured to return from injuries prematurely. The welfare of student-athletes also encompasses advocating for their rights, providing them with platforms to voice concerns, and ensuring they receive a fair share of the rewards that their hard work generates.

The ethical framework in collegiate athletics is a testament to the belief that sports are a vehicle for education, personal development, and societal progress. It is a binding force that holds institutions accountable, ensuring that the timeless values of fairness, equity, and respect are not just upheld, but championed.

Gender Equity and Title IX

One of the most significant ethical pillars in collegiate athletics is gender equity, epitomized by Title IX of the Education Amendments of 1972. This landmark legislation prohibits sex-based discrimination in any school or education program receiving federal funding, compelling athletic programs to provide equal opportunities to male and female student-athletes. The implementation of Title IX has transformed the landscape of collegiate sports, dramatically increasing the participation of women and contributing to a more inclusive and equitable environment. However, the journey towards true gender equity remains ongoing, as institutions continue to grapple with ensuring equal access to resources, funding, and media coverage. This topic will be covered further in the next chapter.

Sportsmanship and Integrity

Sportsmanship and integrity serve as the cornerstones of the ethical framework in collegiate athletics, reflecting the broader educational and developmental goals of sports participation. Sportsmanship is not merely about adhering to the rules of the game but also about embracing a spirit of camaraderie and respect. It's about celebrating victories with humility and accepting defeats with grace. The true test of sportsmanship often comes not when an athlete is ahead, but in moments of adversity and challenge. Collegiate institutions play a pivotal role in cultivating this ethos, integrating it into every facet of their athletic programs. This commitment to sportsmanship ensures that the games played are not only a competition of skills but also an exhibition of character development and ethical growth.

Integrity in competition is equally critical, implying honesty in one's actions and consistency in upholding moral principles regardless of the situation's demands or the potential benefits of unethical behavior.

In collegiate sports, integrity involves a range of actions from ensuring fair play to honest self-representation and the truthful reporting of one's own performance. It's about maintaining one's honor even when opportunities to cut corners present themselves, and it's about coaches and administrators leading by example, creating an environment where ethical behavior is expected, recognized, and rewarded. When integrity is placed at the heart of collegiate athletics, it not only enhances the quality of the competition but also contributes to the authentic development of the student-athletes' character.

However, the pressures of collegiate athletics can sometimes push individuals toward ethical boundaries, whether it's the allure of a championship, the demand for college admission, or the possibility of professional prospects. It is in these high-pressure situations that the true value of sportsmanship and integrity is tested. Coaches, administrators, and athletes alike must resist the temptations of a win-at-all-costs mentality, as the implications of such a mindset can be far-reaching and detrimental. To uphold the true spirit of sportsmanship and integrity, policies and educational programs need to be implemented that emphasize these values. By fostering a culture that prizes ethical behavior and by instituting clear consequences for transgressions, collegiate athletics can strive to be an exemplar of how sports can positively influence personal and social development.

Recruiting Ethics

Recruitment ethics in collegiate athletics play a fundamental role in shaping the landscape of college sports. The process is not simply about building a competitive team but also about the responsible engagement of young athletes within the educational environment. Ethical recruitment begins with the recognition that student-athletes are, first and foremost, students. This means prioritizing their academic and personal development as equally important as their athletic prowess. Recruiters and coaches have a duty to present honest information about the expectations and realities of competing at the collegiate level, including time commitments, academic standards, and the balancing act that comes with being a student-athlete. This truthful dialogue helps prospective athletes make informed decisions that align with their long-term educational and career goals, ensuring a fit that is beneficial for both the student and the institution.

The pressure to win games and secure the best talent often creates a temptation to promise more than can be delivered or to bend the rules of recruitment in favor of gaining a competitive edge. However, maintaining ethical standards requires a steadfast commitment to transparency and fairness. Recruiters should provide a consistent message to all recruits, avoiding the offering of improper benefits or the exertion of undue influence over a student's decision-making process. It's crucial that the recruitment process respects the autonomy of the prospective student-athlete, allowing them to make choices based on their best interests, without feeling coerced or misled. Upholding these ethical standards not only protects the integrity of collegiate sports but also ensures the well-being and satisfaction of the student-athletes once they join the program.

Moreover, the commitment to ethical recruitment extends to the actions taken once a student-athlete commits to a program. This includes honoring scholarship offers, supporting the academic success of student-athletes through tutoring and mentoring programs, and providing resources for their physical and mental health. It's about fostering an environment where student-athletes can thrive in all aspects of their college experience, not just athletically. When coaches and recruiters adhere to these ethical practices, they set the stage for a collegiate athletics environment that is equitable, supportive, and conducive to the holistic growth of the student-athlete. This ethical foundation is what distinguishes collegiate sports as a nurturing ground for not only athletic excellence but also academic achievement and personal development.

Student-Athlete Welfare

Student-athlete welfare is the linchpin of a robust ethical approach in collegiate athletics. It demands that the health, safety, and academic well-being of the individual are placed above the competitive and financial interests of the sports program. Institutions must ensure that student-athletes are not viewed merely as competitors but as individuals with a diverse range of needs and aspirations. Access to quality medical care is non-negotiable, and proactive measures must be in place for injury prevention and management. Academic support structures should be robust, acknowledging the unique time-management challenges faced by student-athletes. Furthermore, mental health resources are essential, providing a support system for athletes to manage the pressure and psychological demands associated with high-level competition and the dual responsibilities of being both a student and an athlete.

The educational institutions and athletic programs carry the responsibility of safeguarding their student-athletes against exploitation. It is their duty to provide a secure environment that promotes fair treatment in all aspects of college athletics. This includes respecting the personal rights of student-athletes, honoring their scholarships and providing them with life skills and career development opportunities that will serve them beyond their collegiate athletic careers. As the lines between amateurism and professionalism in college sports continue to blur, the dialogue surrounding the compensation of student-athletes, particularly in revenue-generating sports, gains momentum. This debate touches upon the ethical consideration of whether and how student-athletes should share in the financial benefits they help to generate. With new regulations allowing student-athletes to profit from their name, image, and likeness (NIL), institutions must navigate this new landscape ethically, ensuring that athletes are fairly compensated while maintaining the integrity of the educational experience.

Addressing student-athlete welfare also means confronting the commercial pressures that can sometimes overshadow the educational mission of collegiate athletics. The balance between running a successful athletic program and maintaining the primary focus on education can be delicate. Student-athletes should not feel that their worth is solely tied to their athletic performance. Instead, institutions must strive to reinforce the value of the student-athlete's personal development, educational success, and overall well-being. The commitment to student-athlete welfare should be evident in every policy and practice, from recruitment through to graduation, underlining the institution's dedication to nurturing not just the athlete, but the individual as a whole.

Ethical Leadership and Accountability

Ethical leadership and accountability within collegiate athletics are vital for fostering an environment that respects the core values of sports and education. Athletic directors, coaches, and administrators are entrusted with the responsibility of not just leading their teams to victory, but also guiding their student-athletes in becoming responsible and ethical individuals. This responsibility is carried out through actions that demonstrate integrity, fairness, and respect for all participants in the athletic process. Leaders in athletics must be transparent in their decisions and open in their communication, ensuring that all actions are aligned with the mission and values of their institutions. They must also be prepared to confront ethical dilemmas, making tough decisions that may not always be popular, but are in the best interest of the student-athletes and the integrity of the sports program.

The principles of ethical leadership extend beyond personal conduct; they also encompass the creation and enforcement of policies that hold all members of the athletic community to high ethical standards. This means establishing clear expectations for conduct, consistent enforcement of rules, and equitable treatment of all athletes. When issues arise, such as allegations of misconduct or breaches of policy, it is imperative that leaders act swiftly and judiciously to address them. Accountability is not only about responding to infractions but also about putting systems in place that minimize the likelihood of their occurrence. This proactivity is the hallmark of ethical leadership and is critical in maintaining the trust and confidence of student-athletes, the campus community, and the public at large.

Governing bodies, such as the NCAA, play a pivotal role in upholding ethical standards within collegiate athletics. These organizations are tasked with creating a regulatory framework that promotes fair play, student-athlete welfare, and the integrity of sports. They must vigilantly monitor compliance with these regulations and impose consequences when violations occur. However, their role is not solely punitive; governing bodies must also provide guidance and support to institutions as they navigate the complex ethical landscape of collegiate athletics. Through a collaborative effort between individual institutions and governing bodies, the shared goal of a collegiate athletic environment that is fair, respectful, and ethically sound can be achieved, safeguarding the welfare of student-athletes and the honor of the games they play.

Discussion Questions

- Discuss the role of sportsmanship and integrity in collegiate athletics. Can you provide examples where these principles were either upheld or violated? What were the consequences of such actions?
- Reflect on the ethical considerations involved in the recruitment of student-athletes. How can colleges and universities ensure that their recruitment practices are both competitive and ethical?
- Explore the ethical obligations of colleges and athletic programs towards the welfare of student-athletes. Consider physical health, academic success, and mental well-being. How can institutions balance these responsibilities with the competitive demands of collegiate sports?
- What characteristics define ethical leadership within collegiate athletic programs? Discuss the importance of accountability in maintaining the integrity of sports programs and protecting the interests of student-athletes.
- How can athletic directors and coaches exemplify ethical leadership in their programs? Discuss the impact of their leadership style on the behavior of student-athletes and the overall ethical climate of the athletic department.
- Athletic scholarships are a significant aspect of collegiate athletics. Discuss the ethical considerations in awarding these scholarships. Should all sports receive equal consideration, or is it ethical to prioritize scholarships for revenue-generating sports?
- The commercialization of collegiate athletics has led to debates about

compensating student-athletes. Discuss the ethical implications of paying student-athletes. Consider the impact on the amateur status of college sports and the potential consequences for non-revenue sports.

- Student-athletes often face health risks, including injuries and mental health issues. Discuss the ethical responsibilities of colleges and athletic departments in ensuring the health and safety of their athletes. How should decisions be made regarding return-to-play protocols for injured athletes?
- Transparency and accountability are crucial for maintaining trust in collegiate athletic programs. Discuss the importance of these principles in the context of financial operations, recruitment practices, and compliance with rules and regulations. How can athletic departments foster a culture of transparency and accountability?

Case Study 8.1: Pony Excess

The landscape of collegiate athletics was shaken in the 1980s when Southern Methodist University (SMU), a private institution with deep community ties through football, faced a crisis that would serve as a stark example of the consequences of unethical behavior in collegiate sports. With its football program already known for early transgressions involving illegal cash subsidies to players, SMU's continual disregard for NCAA rules led to significant penalties, including a suspension from the Southwest Conference.

The Event

The situation reached its zenith when the NCAA imposed what came to be known as the "death penalty" on SMU's football program in 1987. This was due to ongoing infractions that included payments and gifts to players, and the program's inability to detach itself from a well-entrenched system of financial support from boosters. Despite previous sanctions and probations, the program continued to engage in activities that flagrantly violated NCAA regulations, even as the governing body encouraged transparency and cooperation.

The Impact

The "death penalty" had a long-lasting impact on SMU's football program. After being shut down for the 1987 season and with severe limitations upon its return, SMU football suffered nearly three decades of poor performance. The institution's approach to the NCAA's investigations – confrontational and uncooperative – reflected a broader culture of defiance against regulatory authorities, illustrating the profound effects of a leadership void in ethical oversight.

Discussion

- How can an athletic department foster a culture of integrity to prevent such systemic failures?
- In light of SMU's case, what measures should the NCAA consider for future violations to enforce compliance without devastating a program for decades?
- What role does the institution's leadership play in both the development and resolution of such crises?
- How might the balance between punitive actions and rehabilitative support be struck in cases of student-athlete misconduct?
- What systems can be put in place to ensure that athletic success does not override academic integrity and ethical standards?

Case Study 8.2: Concussion Management and Player Safety

A collegiate soccer team, known for its competitive edge and remarkable team spirit, had a challenging season with multiple players sustaining injuries. Among them, a particularly valued player, who had a history of concussions, faced a critical decision point after sustaining yet another head injury during a crucial match.

The Event
During the last game of the regular season, the player collided with an opponent and exhibited signs of a concussion. This was the player's third concussion in the season, and each incident had been progressively more severe. The medical staff followed the institution's concussion management plan, which necessitated the player's immediate removal from the game and a comprehensive evaluation.

The Impact
The team faced a dilemma: allowing the player to continue in the upcoming playoffs could lead to long-term health consequences, but sidelining the player could severely impact the team's championship prospects. The player, fearing the potential end of a burgeoning athletic career, was anxious to return to the field. The situation sparked a heated debate within the athletic department, with concerns about player safety, team success, and the message sent to other student-athletes about the institution's priorities.

Discussion

- Should the welfare of the individual player take precedence over the team's potential success in the playoffs? Why or why not?
- What considerations should guide the decision of the medical staff regarding the player's return to the field, considering the institution's concussion management plan?

- How can the athletic department balance its responsibility to protect its athletes with competitive pressures?
- In what ways does the pressure to perform and win impact ethical decision-making in collegiate athletics?

Chapter 9
Discrimination & Title IX

The realm of intercollegiate athletics, governed predominantly by the NCAA, presents a dynamic yet complex landscape marked by its own set of challenges and opportunities. Among these, issues of discrimination based on gender, race, and disability stand out as significant areas of concern that continue to shape policies, practices, and perceptions within the sector. This chapter delves into these issues, exploring the roots and ramifications of inequity and underrepresentation, while also highlighting the pivotal role of Title IX in fostering an environment of equality and fairness in collegiate sports.

Upon successful completion of this unit, students will be able to:

- Understand the Historical Context of Discrimination in NCAA Sports.
- Analyze the Impact of Title IX on Gender Equity in Sports.
- Identify and Assess Racial and Disability Discrimination Challenges.
- Evaluate Strategies and Policies for Combating Discrimination.
- Develop a Comprehensive Understanding of Equity and Inclusion Principles.
- Apply Knowledge to Advocate for Change.

The Fabric of Discrimination in NCAA Sports

Discrimination within NCAA sports manifests in various forms, directly impacting athletes, coaching staff, and administrative bodies. Gender discrimination, racial disparities, and the challenges faced by athletes with disabilities underscore the complexities of creating an inclusive athletic environment.

Gender Discrimination and Inequity

Gender discrimination within intercollegiate athletics is a persistent issue that extends beyond the playing fields and into the very infrastructure that sustains collegiate sports. Historically, women's sports have been marginalized, receiving a fraction of the attention and funding accorded to men's sports. The allocation of resources has been significantly imbalanced, with men's programs often enjoying superior facilities, equipment, and travel budgets. This disparity is not only reflected in the material aspects but also in the opportunities available to female athletes. Scholarships for women, until the intervention of Title IX, were limited, impeding access to higher education and athletic participation for many talented individuals.

Moreover, gender inequity is starkly apparent in media representation and coverage. Men's sports traditionally dominate television airtime and media coverage, relegating women's sports to the sidelines. This lack of exposure diminishes the perceived value of women's athletics, leading to a cycle of underinvestment and underappreciation. Media portrayal is not only about the quantity of coverage but also the quality, with women's sports often being portrayed in ways that emphasize aesthetics over achievements, further perpetuating gender stereotypes.

Institutional practices within athletic departments also mirror this gender disparity. Leadership roles are overwhelmingly held by men, which has far-reaching implications on decision-making processes and policy formation. The minimal representation of women in these positions results in a lack of advocacy for women's sports programs and can lead to a culture that does not prioritize gender equity. This systemic bias extends beyond the borders of the institutions and reflects a broader societal issue of gender inequality. The battle for equity in collegiate sports is a microcosm of the struggle for gender equality in the wider world, and progress in this arena could herald broader societal change.

Racial Disparities

Racial disparities within the collegiate athletic system are an unfortunate reflection of broader social inequities. Despite the diverse array of talent across the nation, there remains a stark underrepresentation of minority athletes in many non-revenue sports, such as swimming, tennis, and golf. This skewed representation raises concerns about the access to and availability of resources for youth sports in minority communities, which often serve as feeder systems into collegiate athletics. The limited access to quality training facilities, experienced coaches, and developmental leagues in these communities disproportionately affects athletes' abilities to compete at higher levels, creating a compounding effect that extends into college sports.

The recruitment practices for collegiate athletics often underscore the racial disparities prevalent within the system. Predominantly white institutions may prioritize recruitment from areas or schools with higher economic status, which are often less racially diverse, perpetuating a cycle of underrepresentation. Moreover, the implicit biases held by some recruiters can influence their decisions, often at the subconscious level, leading to a preference for certain demographics over others. These biases, coupled with a lack of proactive diversity policies, not only hinder the inclusivity of the recruitment process but also limit the potential pool of talent that could greatly benefit the teams and the NCAA as a whole.

Furthermore, racial disparities are not confined to the athletes alone but are also present in the coaching ranks and administrative structures of collegiate sports. The scarcity of minority coaches and administrators in significant numbers leads to a homogeneity of perspectives that can inadvertently maintain the status quo. Such a lack of diversity in leadership positions fails to reflect the demographic makeup of the student-athlete population and can stifle the voices and concerns of minority athletes. This lack of representation also has a trickle-down effect on institutional policies and the cultural norms within teams and the larger athletic community, perpetuating a non-inclusive culture that struggles to effectively address and rectify these long-standing disparities.

Disability and Accessibility

In the sphere of NCAA sports, athletes with disabilities are often confronted with barriers that go beyond the physical demands of the sport itself. These barriers can range from a lack of wheelchair-accessible facilities to insufficient support services that are critical for their training and competition. Such challenges extend to the recruitment process, where athletes with disabilities may face biases that question their capabilities. The inequitable distribution of resources can also lead to fewer opportunities for these athletes to participate in sports at a collegiate level, thereby denying them the chance to fully engage in the transformative experience of college athletics.

Moreover, the current infrastructure of many collegiate athletic programs falls short in addressing the needs of athletes with disabilities. This can be seen in the minimal availability of adaptive sports programs and the lack of specialized equipment that can facilitate the participation of all athletes. Without these accommodations, the promise of inclusivity remains unfulfilled, restricting access to the benefits of sports participation. Consequently, the NCAA has a crucial role to play in advancing the inclusivity agenda by establishing and enforcing standards that uphold the rights and needs of athletes with disabilities.

To truly champion inclusivity and equal opportunity, concerted efforts must be undertaken to dismantle the existing barriers faced by athletes with disabilities. This includes investing in accessible facilities and equipment, fostering an inclusive culture within athletic departments, and actively promoting adaptive sports programs. Through such measures, NCAA sports can lead by example, demonstrating a commitment to the principles of equity and inclusion that should underpin all athletic endeavors. It is only by embracing this inclusive approach that NCAA sports can fully honor the spirit of competition and camaraderie that lies at the heart of collegiate athletics.

Title IX: A Beacon of Equality

The Title IX of the Education Amendments Act of 1972 states, "No person in the United States shall, on the basis of sex, be excluded from participation in, be denied the benefits of, or be subjected to discrimination under any education program or activity receiving Federal financial assistance." This law applies to any institution that receives federal financial assistance from the U.S. Department of Education. In other words, any educational program, including institutions of higher education, that receive federally appropriated funds have to operate through nondiscriminatory methods.

The groundwork for Title IX started back in October of 1967, as President Lyndon B. Johnson signed Executive Order 11375, which prohibited federal programs and federally funded operations from discriminatory employment methods, specifically on the basis of sex. This executive order laid the groundwork for the future of legislation that dealt with gender equity. This positive momentum continued with Title VII of the Civil Rights Act, which prohibited employment discrimination on the basis of religion, national origin, race, or sex, but this law was not applicable to employment in educational institutions. Likewise, Title VI was created to prohibit discrimination in federally assisted programs, but only on the basis of race, but not sex. The need for federal legislation dealing with discriminatory practices in educational institutions is evident in the following example. During the 1960s in the state of Virginia, there was a three-year period that where over 20,000 women denied college admission to federally funded universities. However, during this very same frame of time, not a single man was denied admission or turned away.

After President Richard Nixon signed the Title IX of the Education Amendments Act into law in June of 1972, society saw near-immediate results, as just seven years after being signed, women enrolled in undergraduate degree-seeking programs outnumbered men, and just three years after that in 1982, women were earning bachelor's degrees at a higher rate than men were for the first time.

Another significant impact of the Title IX of the Education Amendments Act of 1972 was sexual harassment being deemed a form of sex discrimination, thus becoming illegal under Title IX. First used in a court case involving sexual harassment against an educational institution in Alexander v. Yale, the United States Court of Appeals for the Second Circuit decided that sexual harassment of female students can be considered sex discrimination, and was, thus, illegal under Title IX. This case, along with Title IX, has made college and university campuses across the national much safer places and now provides female students with a safe way to report sexual harassments and assaults. In fact, college campuses have Title IX offices that are committed to maintaining educational environments free from discrimination and harassment.

Title IX and Intercollegiate Athletics

When Title IX of the Education Amendments Act was passed into law in 1972, it was not initially designed to specifically address interscholastic and intercollegiate athletics. However, since sports are a major component of most U.S. institutions of higher education, Title IX has applied to numerous aspects of educational sport. Gender equity in college sport became a political and legal issue with the passing of Title IX, therefore, policy to ensure that opportunities exist for both genders was enacted to be fair in delivering opportunities for both men and women.

Despite the NCAA's recent efforts to establish gender equity, the association initially met Title IX with great resistance. After Title IX was first introduced and started to impact intercollegiate athletics, the NCAA did not warmly embrace the federal statute. In fact, the NCAA actually brought the first legal challenge to Title IX in the mid-1970s against Joseph Califano, who, at the time, was serving as the Secretary of the U.S. Department of Health, Education, and Welfare. In 1993, the NCAA Board of Governors established the NCAA Gender Equity Task Force in order to compel more meaningful progress of gender equity at NCAA-member institutions at every level of competition. The NCAA Gender Equity Task Force defines gender equity stating that, "No individual should be discriminated against on the basis of gender, institutionally or nationally, in intercollegiate athletics." The NCAA Gender Equity Task Force further says, "An athletics program can be considered gender equitable when the participants in both the men's and women's programs would accept as fair and equitable the overall program of the other gender."

Three-Prong Test

The primary means by which an institution can demonstrate compliance to Title IX through their respective athletic departments is through the so-called three-prong approach. By law, an athletic department is deemed to be compliant with Title IX is through meeting any one of the following three prongs:

1. Proportionality, or having the same percentage of female athletes and female undergraduates,
2. A continuing history of expanding athletic opportunities for women, and
3. Demonstrating success in meeting the interests and abilities of female students.

Proportionality aims to measure if a university's varsity athletics programs have a number of male and female students enrolled that is proportional to the overall representation of the university's student body. In other words, if a university's student body population is split even at 50% for both male and female students, the athletics programs must also be close to an even 50% split or they would not be compliant with this prong. Instead of cutting men's programs to become compliant, universities are encouraged to add new female teams.

Meeting the second prong, expansion, can be accomplished if a university and its athletics department can show they are expanding their university-sponsored female athletics programs. However, the female athletics expansion must align with the interests of female students , who have shown interest in joining specific athletics programs and teams. If a university athletics department can show they meet these requirements, even if they still don't meet the proportionality requirement, they can be considered Title IX compliant.

The last prong is somewhat of a last resort, as it is only utilized by universities that sponsor fewer programs and opportunities for female students compared to the programs offered to male students, and are not actively expanding. A university can show compliance to this third prong by illustrating they already are meeting students interests. This would require a university to prove they have taken input from female students, by way of surveys, interviews, and focus groups, and showing that these females are substantially satisfied with having less funding and fewer athletic opportunities than their male counterparts.

Critiques of Title IX

Despite many of the great successes of Title IX, since its inception, Title IX's application to intercollegiate athletics has been attacked due to its derivative nature to athletics. As previously stated, Title IX was not initially was not originally designed to address intercollegiate athletics. Because of this, many critics have labeled Title IX to be an unjust quota system that is focused on numbers rather than experiences that limits opportunities for males. Additionally, much scholarly research has shown that many athletic administrators use Title IX as a scapegoat for lavish expenditures for the depleting resources and opportunities that face both men and women participating in intercollegiate athletics. Moreover, the focus on gender discrimination under Title IX has raised concerns about the oversight of racial and disability discrimination within NCAA sports. Advocates for racial equality and disability rights argue for the need to expand protections and to foster a more inclusive environment that addresses all forms of discrimination.

The Impact of Title IX on Women's Sports

The impact of Title IX on women's sports has been both transformative and expansive. Prior to Title IX, women's sports programs were frequently underfunded and undervalued, with limited opportunities for scholarships, competition, and professional coaching. The legislation catalyzed a dramatic increase in women's sports participation at the collegiate level, growing from fewer than 30,000 female college athletes before its enactment to over 200,000 today. Title IX has not only bolstered funding and support for women's athletic programs but also established gender equity as a cornerstone principle within NCAA institutions, mandating equal treatment and opportunity across all areas of athletics from facilities to recruitment.

Beyond the quantifiable growth in participation and program investment, Title IX has profoundly influenced societal perceptions of female athletes and women's sports. The legislation has contributed to a cultural shift that acknowledges the legitimacy and value of women's sports, celebrating female athletic achievements and paving the way for greater media coverage and fan engagement. This shift has extended to a broader societal acknowledgment of women's rights, paralleling the rise of the women's movement and influencing the discourse surrounding gender roles and equality. Title IX has become more than a legal mandate; it represents a commitment to fairness and the dismantling of long-standing barriers, thereby not only leveling the playing field but also inspiring future generations of women to pursue excellence in all realms of athletics and beyond.

Moving Forward: Towards Greater Inclusion and Equity

The journey towards achieving greater inclusion and equity in NCAA sports is ongoing. It requires a multifaceted approach that not only enforces existing regulations like Title IX but also embraces broader initiatives aimed at addressing racial and disability discrimination. While significant strides have been made, particularly through the implementation of Title IX, the journey towards a truly inclusive and equitable athletic environment is far from complete. It demands ongoing effort, introspection, and action from all stakeholders within the NCAA and beyond. Strategies may include increasing diversity in leadership roles, implementing targeted recruitment practices, and enhancing support and resources for athletes from all backgrounds.

Discussion Questions

- How does the historical context of gender discrimination in NCAA sports reflect broader societal patterns of gender bias?
- Discuss the impact that media representation has on the perception and value of women's sports. How can media coverage of women's sports be improved to foster greater equity?
- In what ways do institutional practices within athletic departments contribute to gender disparity, and what measures can be taken to address these issues?
- Examine the role of Title IX in expanding opportunities for women in collegiate sports. Has Title IX been successful in achieving its goals, and what challenges remain?
- How can NCAA sports programs be reformed to better address the needs of athletes with disabilities? Discuss the current barriers and propose solutions.
- Reflect on the importance of diversifying leadership roles within

NCAA sports. Why is it critical for the demographic makeup of leadership to reflect that of the student-athlete population?

- Analyze the strategies mentioned for moving forward towards greater inclusion and equity. Which strategies do you believe will be most effective, and why?
- Critically assess the argument that Title IX may unintentionally limit opportunities for male athletes. Is there a way to achieve gender equity without causing such limitations?
- Discuss the potential ripple effects of achieving gender equality in collegiate sports on wider societal change.

Case Study 9.1: Underrepresentation in Coach and Admin Roles

The struggle for equality and diversity in NCAA athletics has been a persistent challenge, especially regarding the underrepresentation of Black Americans in coaching and administrative roles. This issue reflects a broader societal pattern of racial inequity and has significant implications for the culture and governance of college sports. Despite Black athletes' substantial representation in player statistics, this diversity has not been echoed in leadership positions, which are crucial for shaping the policies and culture of college athletics.

The Event
In 2015, a survey highlighted that only a small percentage of leadership positions in major sports leagues were held by people of color. For example, in baseball, only four general managers were Black – the fewest among the major leagues. The NBA showed a slightly more favorable diversity status, with better representation in executive roles. Yet, these numbers still paint a stark picture of the underrepresentation of minorities in decision-making capacities within sports organizations.

The Impact
The underrepresentation of Black Americans in NCAA coaching and administrative roles has far-reaching implications. It not only affects the opportunities and mentorship available to Black student-athletes but also influences the broader institutional culture, potentially perpetuating a cycle of bias and exclusion. The absence of diverse leadership can limit the perspectives and voices in critical discussions about the direction and values of collegiate athletics programs. Moreover, it challenges the NCAA's commitment to diversity and inclusion, a cornerstone for fostering a fair and progressive athletic environment.

Discussion

- How does the underrepresentation of racial minorities in NCAA coaching and administrative roles reflect systemic issues in the broader context of sports?
- In what ways can increased diversity in NCAA leadership positions improve the collegiate sports culture and benefit student-athletes?
- What are the potential consequences of the ongoing underrepresentation of Black Americans for the future of NCAA sports?
- Discuss the strategies that NCAA could employ to improve diversity in coaching and administrative roles. How effective might these be?
- Reflect on how mentorship programs within collegiate sports can be developed to support the professional growth of minority candidates in administrative and coaching positions.
- Consider the barriers that may prevent litigation as a strategy for addressing underrepresentation. What are alternative ways to address this issue outside of the courtroom?

Case Study 9.2: Equitiable Resources Across Sports

Historically, gender equity in collegiate sports has been a contentious issue, resulting in the implementation of Title IX to ensure equal treatment and opportunities for men and women in educational programs receiving federal financial aid. Despite these efforts, inequities persist, often manifesting in subtle ways that impede true gender parity in athletics.

The Event
In this hypothetical case, Middleton University is facing criticism for its recent renovation of athletic facilities. While the men's football and basketball teams received state-of-the-art upgrades to their training facilities and arenas, the women's teams were allocated substantially less funding, leading to comparatively modest improvements. Additionally, concerns were raised about the inequitable distribution of scholarships, coaching staff support, and prime-time scheduling for games. The women's teams have voiced their frustration, arguing that the institution's actions violate the spirit of Title IX, and they have garnered the support of student bodies and gender equity advocacy groups.

The Impact
The outcry at Middleton University has catalyzed a national conversation about the subtle ways gender inequity persists in collegiate athletics. Many are calling for a reevaluation of Title IX's implementation, demanding more rigorous enforcement and clearer guidelines that go beyond numerical compliance to ensure equality in the quality of resources and support. As the situation unfolds, Middleton University

is being closely watched by other institutions, legal experts, and policymakers who recognize the potential for this case to set a precedent for future Title IX compliance and gender equity initiatives in sports programs nationwide.

Discussion

- How do you perceive the university's allocation of resources to men's and women's sports facilities, and what implications does it have for gender equity?
- In what ways can Middleton University address the concerns raised by the women's teams to move towards true gender equity?
- What measures can the NCAA and educational institutions take to ensure that compliance with Title IX includes equitable treatment and opportunities in all facets, not just in numerical representation?
- How can student bodies and advocacy groups effectively support efforts towards greater gender equity in collegiate athletics?
- Should there be a system in place to regularly audit and publicly report the equity status of athletic programs in educational institutions?
- Discuss the role that media coverage and scheduling play in promoting gender equity in collegiate sports.

Chapter 10
Recruitment and Retention

The recruiting process in college sports is a multifaceted endeavor that involves identifying, engaging, and ultimately securing commitments from high school athletes to play sports at the collegiate level. This process is critical for the success of college sports programs and involves a combination of scouting, communication, and compliance with NCAA regulations.

Upon successful completion of this unit, students will be able to:

- Identify and explain the key stages and components of the recruiting process in college sports, including talent identification, engagement strategies, and compliance with NCAA regulations.
- Describe the role of scholarships and financial aid in the recruitment of student-athletes, and understand the differences between types of scholarships offered.
- Analyze the impact of the NCAA Transfer Portal on student-athlete retention and how it changes the dynamics of college athletics.
- Evaluate the implications of Name, Image, and Likeness (NIL) rules for student-athletes and collegiate sports programs, including the potential benefits and challenges they present.
- Develop strategies for retaining student-athletes, focusing on academic support, athletic development, and positive team dynamics.
- Assess the ethical considerations and potential conflicts involved in recruiting and retaining student-athletes within the framework of NCAA regulations and the evolving collegiate sports landscape.

Identifying Talent

Identifying talent is the critical first step in the recruiting process, laying the foundation for a successful athletic program. Coaches and recruiters dedicate an extensive amount of time and resources to scouting, which includes attending live games, watching showcases, and visiting tournaments. The goal is to evaluate prospects not just on their current skill level, but also on their potential for growth, their fit within the team's strategy, and their ability to adapt to the collegiate level of play. Scouts also spend hours reviewing game tapes, which provide an in-depth look at a player's consistency and performance under different conditions. Consultations with high school coaches offer insights into an athlete's work ethic, coachability, and character — all crucial elements that can influence a recruit's success on and off the field.

As technology continues to evolve, it has become an indispensable tool in the talent identification process. Data analytics now allow coaches to assess player statistics and performance metrics with greater precision, helping to identify hidden gems and understand nuanced aspects of a player's game. Social media platforms have also emerged as a powerful scouting resource, offering real-time access to athlete performances and a more direct communication channel with prospects. Platforms like Twitter and Instagram can showcase an athlete's personality, interests, and personal brand, which are increasingly important in an era where Name, Image, and Likeness (NIL) considerations play a role. Consequently, the savvy use of technology not only enhances traditional scouting methods but also helps in assessing a recruit's marketability and alignment with the program's culture and values.

Engagement and Communication

Once potential recruits have been identified, the engagement process begins. Recruiting student-athletes is governed by a complex set of NCAA regulations designed to ensure fairness among member schools and safeguard the well-being of prospective student-athletes. The NCAA defines prospective student-athletes as individuals who have begun ninth-grade classes, marking the start of their eligibility for recruitment. The rules cover various aspects of recruitment, including permissible contact times and the regulations surrounding official visits, to maintain a balanced competitive field. These regulations not only dictate the timing and frequency of communications through emails, phone calls, and social media but also establish the framework within which institutions engage with potential recruits, ensuring that every interaction aligns with the overarching goal of fairness and transparency.

The engagement process between coaches and potential recruits is carefully regulated to protect the prospects and ensure an equitable recruitment environment. Coaches initiate contact through various channels, abiding by NCAA rules that specify when and how often they can communicate with recruits. This process includes both official and unofficial visits, which are crucial for recruits to gain a firsthand understanding of campus life and team dynamics. Official visits, funded by the institution, and unofficial visits, paid for by the recruits, offer valuable opportunities for in-depth interactions with current team members and coaches. These visits are subject to strict NCAA guidelines, ensuring that all activities and interactions are conducted in a manner that reflects the integrity of the recruitment process.

Furthermore, the NCAA has adapted its regulations to keep pace with technological advancements, acknowledging the significant role of social media in contemporary recruitment strategies. This adaptation includes the extension of permissible communication channels to include modern platforms like Snapchat, reflecting the evolving methods of interaction between coaches and recruits. Restrictions on off-campus contacts and the timing and number of official visits per sport are meticulously outlined, with specific allowances varying by sport, to prevent any undue advantage. The recruitment process is thus a tightly controlled ecosystem, designed to foster an equitable and respectful dialogue between institutions and prospective student-athletes, underlining the NCAA's commitment to maintaining the integrity and fairness of collegiate athletics.

Scholarships and Financial Aid

Athletic scholarships are a central component of the recruiting process, offering prospects the means to cover expenses such as tuition, room and board, books, and even a modest monthly stipend during the school year. Since the NCAA's authorization in 1956, schools have been able to offer these grants-in-aid (GIAs) to attract talented student-athletes based on their athletic prowess. These scholarships, which are counted annually rather than as a "four-year full ride," can also cover additional costs of attendance like supplies and transportation, excluding any amounts received from Pell Grants designed for students in financial need. Moreover, student-athletes can utilize these funds for off-campus housing and board, and for summer courses, provided they have completed at least one term at the institution. The allocation of financial aid is determined annually, with all awards finalized by July 1 preceding the academic year.

The NCAA's scholarship framework aims to maintain equity among programs by limiting the number of scholarships available per sport. It's vital for recruits to grasp the different types of scholarships and the associated conditions. This knowledge equips them to navigate their options and understand the financial implications of their athletic and academic journey. Understanding these constraints and opportunities within the NCAA's financial aid structure is crucial for aspiring collegiate athletes and their families as they make significant decisions about their educational and athletic futures.

Scholarship limits are set to ensure a level playing field among institutions and to promote fairness in recruiting and competition. These limits vary by division (I, II, III) and by sport. NCAA Division III schools, for example, do not offer athletic scholarships, but Division I and II schools do. Here's an overview of scholarship limits for major NCAA sports in Divisions I and II, where athletic scholarships are offered:

NCAA Division I

- Football: The Football Bowl Subdivision (FBS) has a limit of 85 full scholarships per team, while the Football Championship Subdivision (FCS) limits teams to 63 scholarships. The scholarships in FCS can be divided into partial scholarships.
- Men's Basketball: 13 full scholarships per team.
- Women's Basketball: 15 full scholarships per team.
- Baseball: 11.7 scholarships per team, which can be divided among a maximum of 27 players.
- Softball: 12 full scholarships per team.
- Men's Soccer 9.9 scholarships, which can be divided among players.
- Women's Soccer: 14 scholarships, respectively, per team, which can be divided among players.
- Men's Volleyball: 4.5 scholarships per team, which can be divided among players.
- Women's Volleyball: 12 full scholarships per team.

NCAA Division II

- Football: 36 scholarships, which can be divided into partial scholarships among players.
- Men's and Women's Basketball: 10 scholarships which can be divided.
- Baseball and Softball: Baseball teams have a limit of 9 scholarships, while softball teams can offer up to 7.2 scholarships, both of which can be divided among players.
- Soccer: Men's teams are limited to 9 scholarships, and women's teams to 9.9 scholarships, both of which can be divided.

- Volleyball: Women's teams can offer up to 8 scholarships, while men's teams (where the sport is less common) typically follow the Division I limit of 4.5 scholarships.

It's important to note that these numbers represent the maximum number of scholarships allowed and that individual conferences within the NCAA may impose their own limits. Furthermore, not all programs fully fund their scholarship limits due to budgetary constraints. The distribution of scholarships, especially in sports that allow partial scholarships, can significantly impact recruiting strategies and team composition.

Commitment and National Signing Day

The culmination of the recruiting process is when a recruit commits to a college or university. Verbal commitments, while important, are not binding. The formal commitment occurs when the student-athlete signs a National Letter of Intent (NLI), usually on National Signing Day. Signing an NLI ends the recruiting process for the athlete, as it signifies a binding agreement between the student-athlete and the institution.

Compliance with NCAA Regulations

Throughout the recruiting process, adherence to NCAA rules and regulations is paramount. The NCAA enforces strict guidelines on recruiting to ensure fairness and protect prospective student-athletes. Violations can result in penalties for both the institutions and the individuals involved. These regulations encompass a range of activities, including limitations on communication, timing, and the number of recruitment efforts. For example, high school prospects cannot be contacted by college staff before July 1 following their junior year, with phone calls by authorized staff limited to once per week. Additionally, recruiting in football and basketball has specific timeframes for when initial contact can be made. On-campus recruitment activities must also be conducted within reason, with institutions able to cover the actual round-trip transportation costs for official visits, capped at one sponsored visit per school for each prospect. However, recruits can make unlimited visits at their own expense, and recent adaptations to NCAA policy account for the evolving role of social media in recruitment, such as allowing contact via Snapchat.

Compliance with these NCAA regulations during the recruitment process is critical for maintaining the integrity of intercollegiate athletics. The rules are minutely detailed and expansive, covering the permissible times and number of trips for recruitment, among other factors. The aim is to equalize the playing field and to control the influence of wealthier programs that could otherwise use extensive resources to attract top prospects. Member institutions are expected to strictly adhere to these guidelines, including the frequency of communication with recruits and reasonable limits on entertainment expenses during on-campus visits. Such measures ensure a controlled environment for student-athletes, safeguarding the recruitment process against exploitation while maintaining competitive balance among NCAA schools.

Retaining Student-Athletes, the NCAA Transfer Portal, and NIL

Retaining student-athletes in the face of the NCAA Transfer Portal and NIL opportunities necessitates a holistic approach that transcends traditional recruitment. Colleges must provide robust support systems that cater to academic, athletic, and personal development to foster a sense of community and belonging. The advent of the Transfer Portal introduces flexibility for athletes, requiring programs to enhance their environments to retain talent, while NIL agreements demand guidance to balance new financial opportunities with academic and athletic commitments. By focusing on comprehensive support, colleges can create a nurturing environment that not only retains athletes but also prepares them for success beyond their collegiate sports careers.
Academic Support and Engagement

Academic support services play a vital role in retention. Tutoring, study halls, and academic advising help student-athletes balance their rigorous academic and athletic commitments. Engagement with the campus community through service projects and leadership opportunities also fosters a sense of belonging and commitment to the institution.

Athletic Development and Team Dynamics

Athletic development programs are multifaceted, offering support for the physical and psychological well-being of student-athletes. These programs often include comprehensive strength and conditioning regimens designed to enhance athletic performance while minimizing injuries. Nutrition services ensure athletes fuel their bodies correctly for optimal performance and recovery. Sports psychology services play a vital role, too, helping athletes develop the mental resilience and focus needed to excel in their sports and cope with the pressures of competition.

Team dynamics are equally crucial for athletic success and are significantly influenced by the program's culture, which is shaped by coaches and senior athletes. A positive, respectful, and supportive team environment enables each athlete to flourish. The dynamic within a team can affect performance, with strong team cohesion often leading to better individual and group results. Leadership within the team, clear communication, shared goals, and mutual respect are essential components of effective team dynamics, contributing to a cohesive and motivated group.

The NCAA Transfer Portal

The NCAA Transfer Portal, established in 2018, has significantly changed the landscape of student-athlete retention in collegiate sports. It allows athletes to announce their intention to transfer without seeking permission from their current institution, thus giving them greater freedom and control over their athletic careers. This shift towards autonomy has posed a challenge for coaches in retaining talent, compelling institutions to foster an environment that emphasizes the value and well-being of student-athletes and provides clear pathways for their academic and athletic aspirations, in an effort to minimize transfers.

The Transfer Portal serves as a structured and transparent medium for student-athletes who are contemplating a change in their collegiate affiliations. It begins with the athlete notifying their current school's athletic department of their intention to transfer, after which their information is entered into the portal within two business days. This entry acts as an open invitation for other NCAA-affiliated schools to initiate contact, signaling the athlete's interest in exploring other options and starting the recruitment process anew.

However, navigating the Transfer Portal comes with various NCAA-imposed rules and conditions that vary by sport, division, and individual situations. One significant rule change is the one-time transfer rule, which permits athletes to transfer once without having to sit out of competition for a year, subject to meeting specific criteria. This rule aims to reduce the complexities associated with transferring and align the interests of student-athletes with their pursuit of suitable academic and athletic environments.

Ultimately, the NCAA Transfer Portal has revolutionized the transfer process, enhancing the transparency of negotiations between student-athletes and interested programs. It balances the power between institutions and athletes, granting the latter more authority over their career paths while enabling schools to refine their recruitment tactics. With NCAA regulations continuously evolving, it is crucial for student-athletes and their advisors to stay abreast of the latest rules governing the transfer process to navigate it with clarity and informed confidence.

Name, Image, and Likeness (NIL) Rules

The recent modifications to the Name, Image, and Likeness (NIL) rules have significantly altered the collegiate sports landscape, introducing a new dynamic that allows student-athletes to profit from their personal brands. These changes reflect a fundamental shift in NCAA policies, which previously prohibited athletes from receiving any kind of compensation related to their athletic prowess or fame. The transformation in NIL rules provides student-athletes with the rights to monetize their name, image, and likeness, thereby enabling them to engage in endorsement deals, sponsorships, and other partnerships that utilize their personal brand equity without sacrificing their amateur status.

For years, the NCAA maintained stringent rules to uphold the amateurism ideal within college sports. However, the growing financial implications of collegiate athletics, alongside increased legal and public pressure, necessitated a reconsideration of these policies. The updated NIL regulations emerged against a backdrop of state-level legislation that threatened to dismantle the NCAA's restrictions on athlete compensation, prompting the need for a cohesive national standard. Now, student-athletes have the ability to be remunerated for a variety of activities, including social media promotion, public appearances, autograph signings, and product endorsements. They are also permitted to seek representation from agents to manage their business dealings, with the stipulation that these agents cannot procure professional sporting opportunities on their behalf.

The paradigm shift ushered in by NIL rights has compelled institutions and stakeholders to carefully balance the objective of maintaining equitable competition with the recognition of student-athletes' rights to engage in commerce. The practical application of NIL rules is laden with complexities; schools and athletes must navigate state laws and NCAA regulations to ensure that NIL engagements do not endanger athlete eligibility. This demands a robust compliance infrastructure to ensure the fair and transparent application of these rules, with a view to avert potential abuses that could skew recruiting or mar the integrity of amateur sports.

The introduction of NIL rights has redefined the traditional model of amateur sports. It has bestowed upon student-athletes unprecedented opportunities, extending their influence beyond athletic performance to include professional personal branding activities. This transformation obliges all parties involved—student-athletes, educational institutions, lawmakers, and governing bodies—to adapt to the new regulations.

Programs that effectively educate and support their athletes in managing NIL opportunities are likely to enhance the overall student-athlete experience and could see improvements in retention. In this new era, the emphasis on compliance and the ability to leverage NIL opportunities ethically and effectively will be key to the continued success and integrity of collegiate sports programs.

Discussion Questions

- How does the multifaceted nature of college sports recruiting impact the strategies employed by coaches and recruiters when seeking new talent?
- In what ways have advancements in technology altered the traditional methods of scouting and athlete engagement in collegiate sports?
- Considering the NCAA's strict guidelines on recruitment, how can institutions ensure compliance while effectively communicating with potential recruits?
- Discuss the balance NCAA institutions must strike between offering scholarships and maintaining equity among their programs.
- How do the constraints imposed by NCAA scholarship limits influence recruitment strategies and the overall composition of college sports teams?
- In what ways do official and unofficial visits differ, and how do they serve the recruitment process?
- Reflect on the role that the NCAA Transfer Portal and NIL rules play in retaining student-athletes and discuss the strategies institutions can use to adapt to these changes.

Case Study 10.1: The Dynamics of Recruiting and NIL Money

In the ever-evolving landscape of collegiate sports, recruitment strategies have long been a pivotal aspect of building successful athletic programs. Traditionally, this process focused on scouting talent, ensuring academic eligibility, and providing athletic scholarships. However, the introduction of Name, Image, and Likeness (NIL) compensation has added a new dimension to the recruiting paradigm.

The Event
The NCAA's recent amendments to NIL regulations allowed student-athletes to monetize their personal brand for the first time, prompting a significant shift in recruitment strategies. Amidst this backdrop, a star high school quarterback, previously committed to a mid-tier college program, received a lucrative NIL deal from a local business alliance, inciting his last-minute switch to a more prestigious college with a stronger business and marketing program.

The *Impact*

The quarterback's move sparked discussions on the balance between athletic commitments and financial incentives. It also led to calls for more structured NIL guidelines to prevent conflicts of interest and ensure that recruitment decisions remain grounded in athletic, academic, and personal development considerations.

Discussion

- How do NIL agreements influence the decision-making process of recruits and their families?
- What measures can institutions take to integrate NIL opportunities into their recruitment pitches ethically?
- How might the introduction of NIL compensation affect team dynamics and locker room culture?
- In what ways can the NCAA monitor and regulate NIL activities to prevent undue influence on recruiting?

Case Study 10.2: Jane and the Transfer Portal

Jane Doe, a standout sophomore volleyball player at ABC University, has excelled both on the court and in the classroom. Despite her success, she feels disconnected from the team and has grown increasingly dissatisfied with the lack of playing time and the coaching style. With two years of eligibility left, she faces a pivotal decision about her future.

The *Event*

After a particularly challenging season, Jane enters the NCAA transfer portal, signaling her openness to recruitment by other universities. Her action sends ripples through the athletic department at ABC University, as she is a star athlete with significant potential.

The *Impact*

Jane's entry into the portal garners immediate interest from several top programs. ABC University's volleyball team grapples with the potential loss of talent and the impact on team dynamics. Meanwhile, the student-athlete community at ABC University begins discussing the broader implications of the transfer portal on athletes' rights and the traditional college sports model.

Discussion

- How might Jane's experience in the transfer portal reflect larger trends in college sports regarding student-athlete autonomy?
- What steps could ABC University's athletic department take to improve retention rates and address concerns leading athletes like Jane to consider transferring?

- How do transfer decisions impact team cohesion and the distribution of scholarships within athletic programs?
- In what ways might the NCAA transfer portal challenge or reinforce the existing power dynamics between student-athletes and collegiate sports institutions?
- Discuss the ethical considerations for coaches and athletic departments when dealing with student-athletes entering the transfer portal.

Chapter 11
Finances in Collegiate Athletics

In the dynamic and often scrutinized world of collegiate athletics, understanding the financial underpinnings is crucial for administrators, stakeholders, and fans alike. This chapter delves into the multifaceted financial structure of college athletic departments, highlighting the pivotal role of development officers, and the intricate process of revenue sharing within college conferences. The aim is to provide a comprehensive overview that sheds light on the economic challenges and strategies in managing collegiate athletic programs.

Upon successful completion of this unit, students will be able to:

- Understand the diverse sources of funding for college athletic departments, including ticket sales, broadcast rights, and donations.
- Identify the key responsibilities and strategies employed by development officers in securing financial support for collegiate athletic programs.
- Explore the mechanisms of revenue sharing across college conferences and their impact on financial stability and competitive balance.
- Recognize the importance of merchandising and licensing as revenue streams for collegiate athletic departments.
- Examine the ethical considerations and regulatory constraints involved in the financing of collegiate athletics.
- Analyze the challenges faced by collegiate athletic departments in maintaining financial sustainability and equity among sports programs.

Financing College Athletic Departments

College athletic departments operate in a financial ecosystem that's as competitive as the sports they oversee. Financing these departments involves a mix of revenue streams, each with its own set of dynamics and dependencies. The primary sources of funding include ticket sales, broadcast rights, private donations and fundraising, merchandising and licensing, conference revenue sharing, and student fees and institutional support.

Ticket Sales

Ticket sales are often the financial lifeblood of college athletic programs, providing a direct and tangible measurement of fan support and engagement. In high-profile sports like football and basketball, which traditionally attract large crowds, ticket sales can account for a substantial portion of an athletic department's revenue. The income generated from ticket sales not only supports the day-to-day operations but also significantly contributes to the funding of coaching staff salaries, facility maintenance, and other operational expenses. The pricing strategies for tickets may vary, with dynamic pricing models that reflect demand for high-stakes games or traditional flat-rate pricing. Season ticket sales offer a reliable revenue stream and can create a dedicated fan base, while single-game ticket sales might appeal to the casual fan or visiting supporters. Incentives such as priority seating, parking, and bundled packages with merchandise or concessions are often employed to enhance ticket sales.

The success of ticket sales is not solely dependent on team performance; it also hinges on marketing efforts and the overall experience offered to fans. Athletic departments invest heavily in marketing campaigns to boost ticket sales, utilizing traditional media outlets, social media, and community engagement initiatives to attract fans. The fan experience is augmented by the atmosphere of the game day, which includes not only the on-field competition but also pre-game festivities, in-game entertainment, and post-game activities. For students and alumni, attending games is often intertwined with school spirit and tradition, further enhancing the perceived value of purchasing tickets. On the other hand, the rise of high-definition television broadcasts and online streaming services presents a challenge, as fans can now enjoy games from the comfort of their homes, potentially impacting ticket sales. Athletic departments must continuously innovate and enhance the live game experience to draw spectators to the stadium or arena, ensuring a robust revenue stream from ticket sales.

Broadcast Rights

Broadcast rights represent a cornerstone of modern collegiate athletics financing, offering a substantial revenue stream that frequently outstrips ticket sales, especially for schools with the privilege of participating in nationally televised sports. The advent of extensive media coverage has transformed college sports into a highly lucrative industry. Schools and conferences enter into multi-year contracts with television networks and streaming platforms, which provide them with national exposure and significant financial returns. These deals often include not just the rights to broadcast games, but also additional programming such as analysis shows, coach interviews, and other related content. The distribution of these funds can vary; some conferences opt to share the proceeds equally among member institutions, while others distribute based on television appearances or success in national rankings.

Streaming platforms have further expanded (and complicated) the market, allowing fans to watch their favorite teams from anywhere, contributing to an increase in the value of broadcast rights. This digital evolution has necessitated a shift in strategy for collegiate athletic departments and conferences, which now must negotiate broadcast rights that encompass both traditional and online viewership. The digital space allows for targeted advertising and partnerships, offering new opportunities for revenue. For conferences and institutions, these broadcast deals are not just a financial lifeline but also a means of boosting recruitment and enhancing their brand on a national stage. Negotiating such deals requires savvy and foresight, as the landscape of media rights is continuously evolving with the advent of new technologies and viewing habits. Effective management and leveraging of broadcast rights are imperative for the financial health and competitive ability of collegiate athletic programs.

Donations and Fundraising

Donations and fundraising activities are the lifeblood of many collegiate athletic programs, serving as a critical complement to other revenue streams like ticket sales and broadcast rights. Alumni, benefactors, and fans contribute financially, motivated by loyalty, school spirit, and the desire to see their teams succeed. These contributions can take various forms, including one-time gifts, annual donations, or legacy gifts through estate planning. Funds raised through these means are pivotal in supporting student-athlete scholarships, ensuring that talented individuals can afford a college education while competing at high athletic levels. Beyond scholarships, donations also underwrite the construction and refurbishment of facilities, providing athletes with top-tier venues for training and competition. Operational costs, such as travel expenses, equipment upgrades, and staff salaries, are also offset by these philanthropic efforts, enabling programs to function smoothly and compete effectively.

The role of fundraising extends beyond mere financial aspects; it fosters a sense of community and ongoing engagement with the institution. Fundraising campaigns are often spearheaded by development officers who craft compelling narratives around the school's athletic ambitions and needs, creating a sense of shared purpose among the donor community. Special events, personal outreach, and tailored communications are all tools used to deepen relationships with potential donors and to recognize their contributions. The sustainability of many programs, particularly those without substantial broadcast revenue or large ticket sales, relies heavily on successful fundraising. The ability to engage a broad base of supporters and to tap into the network of alumni and local businesses is a skill that can set a program apart, ensuring its growth and longevity in the competitive landscape of collegiate athletics.

Merchandising and Licensing

Merchandising and licensing represent a significant and highly visible component of an athletic department's revenue stream. The allure of college sports, coupled with institutional loyalty, drives the demand for merchandise such as apparel, accessories, and memorabilia. These items not only serve as symbols of support and pride for fans but also function as a substantial source of income for athletic departments. Licensing agreements, which allow manufacturers to use school logos and brands, amplify this revenue. These agreements often involve meticulous negotiation to ensure the institution's brand is properly represented and that the financial terms benefit the athletic programs. The success of merchandising and licensing strategies is closely tied to a team's performance and popularity, making this an inherently variable revenue source.

To optimize this revenue stream, athletic departments often collaborate with marketing professionals to create appealing merchandise that captures the latest trends and fan preferences. This can include limited edition items or co-branded products that tap into current cultural moments or achievements on the field. Moreover, the rise of online shopping has expanded the potential market for collegiate merchandise beyond local campus stores, providing a global platform for sales. Strategic online marketing campaigns, utilizing social media and targeted advertising, can significantly boost this revenue stream. For many fans, purchasing and wearing merchandise is a key part of the fan experience, making it imperative for athletic departments to continuously innovate and refresh their merchandise offerings to keep fans engaged and invested in the brand.

Conference Revenue Sharing

Conference revenue sharing is a system designed to support financial equality and competitive balance within collegiate athletic conferences. Through this system, revenues generated from conference-wide media deals, postseason play, and other collective agreements are distributed among member institutions. This communal approach to revenue ensures that even schools that may not have the exposure or success of their higher-profile counterparts still receive a piece of the financial pie. Media deals, often the most lucrative source of shared revenue, are typically negotiated by the conference on behalf of its members, with the proceeds then allocated across the conference according to predetermined agreements. This system allows smaller programs to benefit from the exposure and success of larger ones, promoting a more level playing field where all members can competitively recruit and build their athletic programs.

Revenue sharing extends beyond media deals to include earnings from postseason tournaments, bowl games, and championships, which are significant events that generate considerable revenue through ticket sales, sponsorships, and broadcast rights. These funds are shared among member institutions, bolstering their athletic budgets and enabling investments in facilities, staff, and student-athlete development. The specifics of these revenue-sharing agreements can greatly impact the strategic decisions of athletic departments, influencing everything from scheduling to conference alignment decisions. As the landscape of college sports continues to evolve, with new broadcasting platforms and changing viewer habits, conferences must also adapt their revenue-sharing models. These adaptations must maintain fairness and competitive balance, ensuring the continued success and sustainability of their member institutions' athletic programs.

Student Fees and Institutional Support

Student fees and institutional support constitute another avenue through which collegiate athletic departments may receive funding, albeit one that is frequently debated. Many universities allocate a portion of mandatory student fees to finance their athletic programs, thereby ensuring a stable, albeit sometimes controversial, source of funding. This financial support can cover a range of athletic department needs, from operational costs to facility upgrades and even support for non-revenue sports that might not otherwise be sustainable. Institutional support also comes in the form of direct subsidies, where the university budget includes allocations for the athletic department.

This form of support underscores the institution's commitment to athletics as part of the overall educational experience. However, the use of student fees and institutional funds is often contested, with critics arguing that it diverts resources from academic programs and places an undue financial burden on students. Proponents, however, assert that a vibrant athletic program enriches campus life, enhances the institution's visibility, and can contribute to a more dynamic and comprehensive collegiate experience. The balance between these views is delicate, with each institution determining the extent and nature of support based on its unique circumstances, priorities, and the values of its stakeholders.

Role of Development Officers

Development officers in collegiate athletics play a crucial role as architects of fundraising strategies, fostering relationships with alumni, donors, and corporate sponsors to secure the financial resources necessary for program sustainability and growth. They are tasked with the essential functions of identifying potential funding sources, orchestrating donation campaigns, and ensuring that benefactors are recognized and engaged, thereby laying the groundwork for future support. Specific responsibilities of development officers include building relationships, leading fundraising campaigns, and spearheading stewardship initiatives.

Building Relationships

In the realm of collegiate athletics, development officers shoulder the important task of building and nurturing lasting relationships with a diverse array of stakeholders, including alumni, donors, and corporate sponsors. These professionals employ a blend of interpersonal acumen and strategic communication to cultivate a sense of community and investment among these groups, ensuring a steady flow of support for athletic programs. They are the human touchpoint between the institution and its supporters, working tirelessly to align the interests and passions of alumni and donors with the needs and goals of the athletic department. By recognizing and valuing the contributions of each stakeholder, development officers create a robust network of support that transcends financial transactions, fostering a deeply rooted culture of generosity that can sustain athletic programs through fluctuating economic climates.

Fundraising Campaigns

Fundraising campaigns are pivotal initiatives within collegiate athletics, orchestrated by development officers to secure necessary funds for targeted projects that often include facility renovations, new construction, and endowments for athletic scholarships. Development officers leverage a strategic mix of events, personal appeals, and marketing tactics to reach potential donors, articulating the tangible benefits and long-term impact of their contributions on the athletic programs. These campaigns are not only about meeting immediate financial goals but also about casting a vision for the future of the athletics department, one that potential donors can envisage and feel compelled to support. Effective fundraising campaigns require meticulous planning, a compelling message, and the ability to connect donors' interests with the institution's athletic ambitions. This synergy ensures that funds are raised not only to meet the burgeoning needs of current programs but also to lay a strong foundation for the development and success of future athletic endeavors.

Stewardship

Stewardship in the context of collegiate athletics is a critical function of development officers, who are tasked with ensuring that donors are not only acknowledged for their generosity but also fully aware of the difference their contributions make. This involves creating and sustaining a transparent communication channel where donors receive updates on how their funds are being used, the progress of projects they've supported, and the achievements of student-athletes who benefit from their scholarships. By providing regular, impact-focused reports and opportunities for donors to engage with the institution and its athletes, development officers foster an environment where donors feel connected to and invested in the success of the athletic programs. This sense of shared accomplishment and purpose is essential for cultivating long-term relationships with donors and establishing a culture of philanthropy that encourages ongoing support and new contributions, forming the backbone of a self-renewing funding ecosystem for collegiate sports programs.

Challenges and Considerations

The fiscal landscape of collegiate athletics presents a labyrinth of challenges and considerations that athletic departments must deftly navigate. Financial sustainability is foremost among these challenges, as departments strive to create a stable economic model amidst the ebb and flow of various revenue sources such as donor contributions, ticket sales, and broadcast rights, which can fluctuate with team performance and market trends. This unpredictability necessitates strategic financial planning and diversification of revenue streams to ensure long-term viability. Equity is another pressing issue, where departments must balance the budgetary demands of high-profile sports, often the face of a school's athletic prowess, with the needs of less prominent, non-revenue generating sports. This balancing act is crucial not just for financial fairness but also for fostering inclusivity and diversity within the athletic programs.

Compliance presents an ongoing operational challenge, requiring departments to stay abreast of and adhere to a myriad of NCAA regulations, conference rules, and institutional policies that govern financial practices, including scholarship distributions. Navigating these regulations demands diligence and often a dedicated compliance staff, as the consequences of infractions can be severe, ranging from financial penalties to reputational damage. In addition to these primary concerns, departments must also consider the impact of their financial decisions on student-athletes' academic experiences, community relationships, and the overall integrity of the athletic program. Ultimately, the successful management of collegiate athletics finances hinges on an integrated approach that aligns fiscal responsibility with the core values and mission of the educational institution.

Discussion Questions

- How do fluctuating revenue sources impact the long-term financial planning of collegiate athletic departments?
- Discuss the ethical implications and potential consequences of using student fees to support athletic programs.
- How might the balance between generating revenue and maintaining competitive equity shape the future of collegiate athletics?
- In what ways do development officers play a critical role in aligning donor interests with the goals of the athletic department?
- What strategies can athletic departments employ to navigate the complexities of NCAA regulations and maintain compliance?
- Reflect on the relationship between the success of merchandising and licensing efforts and a team's performance. How does this affect revenue stability?

Case Study 11.1: Alumni Donation

Collegiate athletics operate within a complex financial ecosystem, requiring athletic departments to navigate multiple revenue streams and balance their budgets while ensuring program sustainability and compliance with regulatory bodies. These departments rely on funding from ticket sales, broadcast rights, donations, merchandising, licensing, conference revenue sharing, and, in some instances, student fees and institutional support. Development officers play a pivotal role in fundraising efforts, fostering relationships with alumni, benefactors, and fans to secure financial backing for the department's various needs. Amid these dynamics, the departments face challenges related to financial sustainability, equity among sports programs, and compliance with NCAA regulations.

The Event

A small college known for its academic excellence but with a relatively underfunded athletic program receives a transformative gift from a group of alumni motivated by school spirit and the desire to enhance the college's athletic competitiveness. The gift is intended for the endowment of scholarships for student-athletes and the upgrade of athletic facilities. Concurrently, the college's conference negotiates a new television deal that significantly increases broadcast revenue for member schools, offering an unexpected boost to the college's athletic funding.

The Impact

The alumni gift and increased conference broadcast revenues have a multifaceted impact on the college's athletic department. Firstly, the endowment for scholarships enables the recruitment of talented student-athletes who also align with the college's academic standards, elevating the competitiveness of its teams. Secondly, the facility upgrades attract attention, improving fan engagement and potentially increasing ticket sales for future seasons. Thirdly, the broadcast revenue provides a steady income stream, allowing the department to plan more confidently for long-term investments in its programs.

With the financial boost, the athletic department focuses on equitable distribution of resources, ensuring that both revenue-generating and non-revenue sports benefit from the increased funding. This approach fosters a more inclusive athletic program and enhances the student-athlete experience across all sports. However, the department also faces the challenge of maintaining this financial balance while adhering to NCAA regulations and managing expectations from the college community and stakeholders regarding the use of the new funds.

Discussion

- How should the athletic department prioritize its spending following the influx of funds from the alumni gift and increased broadcast revenues to benefit both the department and the college at large?
- In what ways can the department leverage the facility upgrades to

maximize future revenue opportunities, such as hosting events or improving the game-day experience for fans?

- Considering the potential for fluctuating broadcast revenues and the finite nature of the alumni gift, what strategies should the department implement to ensure financial sustainability over the long term?
- How can the development officers continue to engage donors and the alumni to sustain fundraising momentum following such a significant gift?
- What measures can the athletic department take to ensure compliance with NCAA regulations and ethical considerations in the allocation of the new funds, particularly in regards to scholarships and facility upgrades?
- Reflect on the role of conference revenue sharing in the financial stability of smaller athletic programs. How can these programs maximize the benefits of such arrangements while maintaining competitive equity within the conference?

Case Study 11.2: Maximizing Ticket Sales

In collegiate athletics, ticket sales represent a crucial revenue stream, directly reflecting fan engagement and support for the sports programs. Athletic departments often rely on ticket revenue to fund a significant portion of their operations, including coaching staff salaries, facility maintenance, and athletic scholarships. However, the dynamics of ticket sales can be influenced by a variety of factors, including team performance, marketing efforts, and the overall fan experience at games. The challenge for athletic departments is to maximize ticket sales through effective pricing strategies, promotional efforts, and enhancements to the game-day experience, all while navigating fluctuations in team performance and competition from other entertainment options.

The Event
A mid-tier university with a strong basketball program experiences a sudden decline in ticket sales despite the team's continued success on the court. The decline is initially puzzling to the athletic department, prompting an investigation into potential causes. It's discovered that the drop in sales is attributed to several factors: an outdated ticketing system that makes purchasing and managing tickets cumbersome, a lack of targeted marketing efforts to engage younger fans, and competition from increasing quality of home entertainment options. In response, the athletic department launches a multifaceted initiative to revitalize ticket sales. This includes upgrading to a modern, user-friendly online ticketing platform, implementing dynamic pricing models, and enhancing the game-day experience with new entertainment options and better amenities.

The Impact

The overhaul of the ticketing system leads to an immediate improvement in customer satisfaction, making it easier for fans to purchase and manage tickets, resulting in an uptick in season ticket renewals and new sales. The introduction of dynamic pricing allows the department to adjust ticket prices in real-time based on demand, increasing revenue from high-demand games while also offering more accessible pricing for less popular matchups, thus attracting a broader audience. Enhanced marketing efforts, particularly through social media and digital platforms, successfully engage younger fans, leading to a noticeable increase in student and young alumni attendance. Improvements to the game-day experience, including upgraded facilities and new entertainment options, further boost ticket sales by offering a more enjoyable and immersive experience for all fans.

Discussion

- How can collegiate athletic departments continuously adapt their ticket sales strategies to respond to changing fan behaviors and expectations?
- What role does technology play in modernizing the ticket sales process, and how can departments ensure they are leveraging the latest advancements?
- In what ways can dynamic pricing be utilized to maximize revenue without alienating the fan base, particularly students and long-time supporters?
- How can enhanced game-day experiences contribute to ticket sales growth, and what innovative strategies can be employed to keep fans engaged?
- What metrics or indicators should athletic departments monitor to evaluate the effectiveness of their ticket sales strategies and make data-driven decisions?
- Reflect on the balance between maximizing ticket revenue and maintaining accessibility for fans. How can departments ensure their strategies are inclusive and foster a strong sense of community among supporters?

Chapter 12
NCAA Compliance

NCAA compliance represents a pivotal aspect of the complex and multifaceted world of collegiate athletics. Ensuring adherence to the National Collegiate Athletic Association's rules and regulations is crucial for maintaining the integrity of college sports and ensuring a level playing field. This chapter delves into the intricacies of NCAA compliance, exploring its foundations, challenges, and the impacts on institutions, athletes, and the broader landscape of intercollegiate athletics.

Upon successful completion of this unit, students should be able to:

- Identify the key components of NCAA compliance and their importance in maintaining the integrity of collegiate athletics.
- Analyze the challenges and implications of the commercialization of college sports on NCAA compliance and amateurism.
- Describe the impact of technology and social media on NCAA compliance efforts and the strategies used to address these challenges.
- Evaluate the effects of high-profile NCAA violations on athletic programs, institutions, and the governance of college sports.
- Discuss the evolving landscape of athlete rights, including NIL legislation, and its implications for NCAA compliance and the traditional amateur model.
- Propose adaptive compliance strategies that accommodate changes in athlete compensation while preserving the educational and competitive ethos of collegiate sports.

Foundations of NCAA Compliance

The bedrock of NCAA compliance is rooted in the mission to protect student-athletes' welfare while fostering an environment where academic and athletic experiences can thrive in harmony. The NCAA's stringent regulatory framework encompasses detailed provisions on eligibility, which dictate the academic credentials and amateur status necessary for participation in collegiate sports. Moreover, the rules governing recruiting practices and scholarship awards are engineered to ensure equity and fairness in the treatment of student-athletes. These compliance structures are integral to preserving the educational primacy of the student-athlete experience and preventing the undue influence of athletics on admission decisions.

Within this regulatory landscape, compliance offices embedded in collegiate athletic departments serve as navigators and guardians of institutional integrity. These offices are not merely watchdogs; they also serve an educational function, disseminating knowledge of NCAA rules among coaches, staff, and athletes to foster a culture of compliance. Through proactive monitoring and regular audits of sports programs, these offices work diligently to mitigate the risk of infractions that can lead to sanctions. Their efforts are pivotal in maintaining the equilibrium between the competitive zeal of college sports and the overarching educational values that the NCAA champions.

Challenges in NCAA Compliance

The shifting terrain of college sports is marked by a constellation of pressures that continually test the robustness of NCAA compliance frameworks. The rapid commercialization of collegiate athletics has brought about an intensifying debate around the principles of amateurism, challenging long-standing traditions that delineate the amateur from the professional athlete. Revenue-generating sports have particularly felt the strain, as calls for athlete compensation have gained momentum against the backdrop of lucrative broadcasting deals and sponsorship agreements. The complexities of these economic factors pose intricate challenges for compliance departments, which must reconcile the growth of commercial interests with the foundational tenets of amateur sportsmanship and the fair allocation of resources within athletic programs.

Furthermore, technological advancements and the proliferation of digital platforms have introduced a new realm of compliance considerations. Social media, in particular, has transformed the ways in which athletes and institutions engage with the public and each other. Recruitment, a critical area in collegiate sports, is now navigated through the minefield of online interactions, where compliance officers must remain vigilant to prevent impermissible contact or the untimely release of information. The monitoring of athletes' online presence, while respecting their personal freedom and privacy, adds another layer of complexity to the compliance equation, necessitating sophisticated strategies to educate athletes and staff on best practices in the digital sphere.

These challenges are compounded by the constant flux in societal attitudes and legal perspectives. The evolving discourse on student-athletes' rights, epitomized by legal disputes over the NCAA's rules, requires compliance departments to adapt swiftly to legislative changes and court rulings. As such, compliance efforts are not just about maintaining the status quo but also about anticipating and shaping policy in response to the shifting legal landscape. This environment of continuous change calls for agile and forward-thinking compliance strategies that can accommodate the multifaceted demands of governing bodies, educational institutions, athletes, and the broader community invested in the integrity of collegiate sports.

NCAA Compliance in the Era of Athlete Empowerment

The landscape of NCAA compliance is undergoing a transformative shift as the concept of athlete empowerment gains legal and public support. The crux of this shift is the rights of student-athletes to profit from their name, image, and likeness (NIL), challenging the NCAA's longstanding amateurism model. The change has been catalyzed by high-profile legal battles and state-level legislative actions, with some laws already in effect, granting these new freedoms. This sea change is not only a victory for student-athletes advocating for a share in the revenue they help generate but also a signal for compliance departments to evolve. They must now create policies that harmonize with these developments, ensure athletes can capitalize on their NIL without compromising NCAA eligibility, and manage potential conflicts with existing institutional sponsorship agreements.

The recognition of NIL rights marks a significant move toward balancing the scales between the commercial aspects of NCAA sports and the rights of the athletes. This move, however, introduces complex dynamics into the compliance ecosystem. Compliance officers are tasked with devising systems that protect the institution's interests and oversee the burgeoning market for student-athletes' endorsements and partnerships. They must navigate the interplay between individual athlete endorsements and team or university sponsorship deals, preventing conflicts while upholding contractual obligations. Educational programs aimed at informing athletes about contract negotiations, market value assessments, and the impact of NIL activities on personal and team branding are now crucial components of compliance operations.

Moreover, this era of athlete empowerment necessitates a reevaluation of the very essence of collegiate sports' educational and competitive ethos. As student-athletes emerge as more autonomous market participants, compliance strategies must consider the implications for team cohesion, equity across sports, and the holistic development of the athlete beyond the playing field. Ensuring that the pursuit of NIL opportunities does not detract from academic commitments or create inequities among athletes becomes a delicate balancing act. Compliance frameworks must be agile enough to support student-athletes' entrepreneurial endeavors while preserving the core values that make collegiate sports a unique and valuable facet of the American educational system.

The Academic Progress Rate (APR)

The NCAA Division I Academic Progress Rate (APR) is a cornerstone in the landscape of collegiate athletics, encapsulating the dual aspirations of athletic success and academic achievement among student-athletes. Introduced in 2003 as part of a broader academic reform initiative by the NCAA, the APR stands as a testament to the organization's commitment to fostering an environment where academic success is as paramount as athletic prowess. This reform was devised to enhance the graduation rates and academic standing of student-athletes, thereby aligning the athletic pursuits with the educational missions of member institutions.

Central to the APR's methodology is a team-based metric that meticulously evaluates the academic performance and persistence of student-athletes on a term-by-term basis. This system is ingeniously designed to allocate up to four points per student-athlete each academic term, with points awarded for maintaining eligibility to compete and for continued enrollment at the institution. The aggregate of these points, when normalized against the total possible points and multiplied by 1,000, yields the APR score of a team. This scoring mechanism is not merely quantitative but serves as a reflective measure of a team's commitment to nurturing the academic development of its athletes.

The NCAA has set a benchmark APR score of 930, indicative of a 50% graduation rate, as a minimum standard for teams to circumvent penalties. This threshold underscores the NCAA's resolve in ensuring that student-athletes are not only seen as athletes but as students first, whose academic progress is integral to their collegiate experience. Teams failing to meet this standard may face a spectrum of penalties, ranging from reductions in practice times and scholarship limitations to postseason bans and restrictions on NCAA membership. Such measures underscore the seriousness with which the NCAA views academic accountability and are intended to incentivize institutions to prioritize the academic welfare of their student-athletes.

Beyond its role as a compliance tool, the APR is pivotal in promoting a culture that values and rewards academic achievement alongside athletic excellence. It compels institutions to provide the necessary academic support to their student-athletes, ensuring a balanced approach to their development that prepares them for life beyond sports. The APR's flexibility, demonstrated through the provision for adjustments or waivers, acknowledges the complexities and dynamic nature of college athletics. This flexibility allows for a fair assessment of teams' academic performance, taking into consideration the impact of transfers and unforeseen departures.

The NCAA Division I Academic Progress Rate is a critical mechanism in the ongoing endeavor to harmonize the athletic and academic aspirations of student-athletes. By holding teams accountable for both the academic eligibility and retention of their athletes, the APR illuminates the path towards a collegiate athletic system that values academic success as much as athletic achievement. It is a clear indicator of the evolving priorities within collegiate athletics, where success is not solely measured by victories on the field but also by the academic growth and graduation rates of student-athletes. Through the APR, the NCAA reaffirms its dedication to ensuring that student-athletes are afforded every opportunity to excel academically, thereby enriching their collegiate experience and preparing them for the challenges and opportunities that lie ahead.

The Graduation Success Rate (GSR)

The NCAA Graduation Success Rate (GSR) stands as a pivotal development in the realm of collegiate athletics, offering a refined lens through which the academic achievements of student-athletes are assessed. Introduced to address the limitations of the federal graduation rate, the GSR embodies a more inclusive and accurate measure of student-athlete success, marking a significant stride toward ensuring academic as well as athletic excellence within Division I programs.

Central to the GSR's methodology is its holistic approach to accounting for the academic journeys of student-athletes, including those who transfer between institutions or enroll mid-year. Unlike the federal graduation rate, the GSR integrates transfer students and mid-year enrollees into its analysis, ensuring that the academic progress of a broader spectrum of student-athletes is captured. This inclusion is crucial, recognizing the dynamic nature of student-athlete experiences and the various paths they may take toward academic and athletic fulfillment.

The GSR also distinguishes itself by not penalizing institutions for student-athletes who depart in good academic standing. This nuanced consideration acknowledges the diverse reasons student-athletes may have for transferring or leaving early, such as pursuing professional careers or opportunities at other academic institutions. By focusing on those who graduate within six years of initial enrollment and adjusting for eligible transfers and departures, the GSR offers a more forgiving and comprehensive standard of measurement. This approach not only provides a clearer picture of student-athlete academic success but also promotes a supportive environment conducive to their academic and athletic growth.

The calculation of the GSR begins with the federal cohort of first-time, full-time freshmen and includes incoming athletes receiving athletic aid for the first time. From this cohort, the GSR methodically excludes athletes who leave the institution in a condition that would have allowed them to compete had they returned, thereby refining the cohort to more accurately reflect the institution's role in supporting student-athlete graduation. This calculation, thereby, yields a proportion of student-athletes who graduate or leave in good standing, offering insight into the effectiveness of institutional support systems in fostering academic success among its athletes.

The introduction of the GSR underscores the NCAA's commitment to balancing the dual objectives of athletic competition and academic achievement. By accounting for the unique circumstances of student-athletes, including transfers and early professional departures, the GSR encourages institutions to invest in the holistic development of their athletes, ensuring they are not only prepared for success in their respective sports but are also equipped with the educational foundation necessary for life beyond athletics.

In comparison to the federal graduation rate, which narrowly tracks students graduating from their initial institutions without considering transfers, the GSR provides a more nuanced and comprehensive assessment of student-athlete graduation outcomes. The federal method's limitations often result in a portrayal of student-athlete academic success that falls short of reality, underscoring the significance of the GSR in offering a more accurate and inclusive picture.

The NCAA's Graduation Success Rate represents a forward-thinking approach to evaluating the academic success of student-athletes, reflecting a broader commitment to ensuring their well-being and success both on and off the field. By incorporating the academic trajectories of transfer students and those who leave in good academic standing, the GSR not only elevates the standard for academic measurement but also champions the cause of comprehensive educational support for student-athletes, reinforcing the NCAA's dedication to fostering environments where academic and athletic excellence can flourish in tandem.

Discussion Questions

- How do the principles of NCAA compliance align with the broader goals of higher education and the student-athlete experience?
- What are the potential implications of the growing commercialization of college sports for NCAA compliance and the concept of amateurism?
- How can compliance offices effectively navigate the challenges presented by social media and technology in the context of NCAA regulations?
- In what ways might the changing legal and legislative landscape regarding athlete compensation impact NCAA compliance efforts and the structure of college sports?
- How might the APR influence the behavior of coaches and athletic departments in terms of recruiting and supporting student-athletes, and do you believe this influence positively aligns with the overall academic mission of higher education institutions?
- Considering the intent behind the NCAA's Graduation Success Rate (GSR) to provide a more accurate reflection of student-athletes' academic achievements, how do you think the GSR affects the way athletic programs prioritize academic support services, and what further steps could institutions take to ensure the GSR remains a true indicator of a student-athlete's success post-graduation?

Case Study 12.1: USC & Reggie Bush

Analyzing specific cases of NCAA violations offers valuable insights into the consequences of non-compliance and the importance of robust oversight mechanisms. High-profile cases often result in sanctions such as scholarship reductions, postseason bans, and financial penalties. These repercussions not only affect the competitive capabilities of sports programs but can also tarnish the reputation of institutions and lead to broader debates about the governance of college sports, such as the scandal involving the University of Southern California football program in the early 2000s. USC has a storied athletic history and boasts a strong football program. In the early 2000s, USC was a dominant force in college football, winning multiple championships and individual player awards.

The Event

In 2010, the NCAA concluded a four-year investigation into the USC athletics program, particularly the football team. The investigation focused on allegations that Reggie Bush, a former USC football star who won the Heisman Trophy in 2005, and his family had received improper benefits from sports marketers during his time at USC. These benefits included a limousine ride to the Heisman Trophy ceremony, a rent-free home, and a new car. Under NCAA rules, student-athletes and their families are prohibited from receiving such benefits.

The Impact

The NCAA found that USC had violated numerous compliance rules and imposed severe sanctions on the football program. These sanctions included a two-year postseason ban, the loss of 30 scholarships over three years, and the vacating of all wins from the 2005 season, including the national championship. Reggie Bush voluntarily forfeited his Heisman Trophy, and the NCAA mandated that USC permanently dissociate from Bush. The university also faced reputational damage, and the sanctions had long-term impacts on the program's competitiveness.

Discussion

- How do you think the culture of a successful athletic program might contribute to compliance violations, and what steps should university leadership take to prevent such a culture from developing?
- What role do you believe the NCAA should play in monitoring and enforcing compliance among its member institutions, and are their punitive measures effective in deterring violations?
- Discuss the potential impacts of NCAA sanctions not only on the involved athletes and programs but also on stakeholders such as fans, future recruits, and other student-athletes.
- Should student-athletes have the right to appeal NCAA sanctions individually, particularly in cases where they might face personal consequences, such as the revocation of awards or records?

Case Study 12.2: The Impact of NIL Legislation on NCAA Compliance

The landscape of collegiate athletics experienced a seismic shift with the introduction of Name, Image, and Likeness (NIL) legislation across various states. This groundbreaking development allowed student-athletes to monetize their personal brand for the first time, endorsing products, engaging in promotions, and participating in other money-generating activities related to their NIL. Previously, such opportunities were strictly prohibited under NCAA regulations, maintaining a firm stance on amateurism and the non-commercialization of student-athletes.

The Event

The NIL legislation was introduced when states began to pass laws that contradicted NCAA rules, effectively forcing the hand of the NCAA to adapt or face the possibility of losing its authority over the issue. Some states enacted laws allowing student-athletes to profit from their NIL, while others awaited federal legislation for a unified approach. The NCAA, in response, had to temporarily suspend its NIL rules to permit athletes to engage in activities that would not affect their eligibility, causing a ripple effect across institutions nationwide.

The Impact

The introduction of NIL legislation challenged NCAA compliance offices to quickly adapt their policies and develop new strategies to support student-athletes. The immediate impact was felt in compliance departments, which had to pivot to provide education on personal branding, contract law, and financial management to student-athletes. Long-term implications for the collegiate athletic model include potential disparities in recruiting, the risk of pay-for-play scenarios, and the blurring lines between amateur and professional status.

Discussion

- How can NCAA compliance offices ensure that student-athletes are fully informed and capable of navigating the complexities of NIL agreements without jeopardizing their eligibility or educational outcomes?
- What strategies can institutions implement to balance the commercial interests of student-athletes with the traditional values of collegiate sports and team dynamics?
- In what ways might the NIL legislation affect the recruitment process, and how should compliance offices prepare to address these changes?
- Considering the potential for income disparity among athletes in different sports and genders, what measures can be taken to promote fairness and equity in NIL opportunities?
- How could the NCAA and its member institutions redefine the concept of amateurism in light of NIL legislation, and what might be the long-term effects on the collegiate sports model?
- What safeguards should be established to protect student-athletes from exploitation in NIL activities, and who should be responsible for enforcing these safeguards?

Chapter 13
Academic Support for Student-Athletes

Academic support for student-athletes encompasses a wide array of services and initiatives designed to assist athletes in balancing their academic responsibilities with their athletic commitments. The unique challenges faced by student-athletes, who must manage time effectively, adhere to NCAA academic standards, and still perform at their peak in sports, necessitate a robust support system to ensure their academic and athletic success.

Upon successful completion of this unit, student will be able to:

- Identify the unique academic challenges faced by student-athletes and the necessity for tailored academic support services.
- Describe the components of effective academic support programs for student-athletes, including academic advising, tutoring, and life skills development.
- Evaluate the impact of NCAA academic standards on student-athlete academic performance and eligibility.
- Analyze case studies of successful academic support programs for student-athletes to identify best practices.
- Discuss strategies for overcoming common challenges in providing academic support to student-athletes, such as funding and stigma.
- Explore the role of academic support services in preparing student-athletes for post-college careers and life beyond sports.

Understanding the Student-Athlete

Understanding the unique predicament of student-athletes begins by acknowledging the high-pressure environment in which they operate. Balancing academic coursework and athletic training, these individuals are constantly navigating between two demanding worlds. The pressure to excel is omnipresent, as success on the field can be as highly valued as academic achievement. The intense schedule of a student-athlete can lead to a high-stress lifestyle that demands exceptional time management skills. This juggling act is complicated by the NCAA's academic requirements, which ensure student-athletes must maintain a certain grade point average and course load to remain eligible to compete.

However, the challenges of academic performance are often amplified for student-athletes. They may face additional difficulties such as missed classes due to travel for games, fatigue impacting study habits and concentration, and the significant time required for practice, training, and competition. These factors can lead to academic underperformance, not necessarily due to a lack of ability or dedication, but because of the sheer difficulty in balancing these two aspects of their collegiate experience. It's a nuanced struggle that requires understanding and support from coaches, academic advisors, and faculty to navigate successfully.

To truly support student-athletes, institutions must develop a robust support system that is responsive to the pressures these students face. This system should encompass academic advising tailored to accommodate their unique schedules, tutoring services that understand the demands of athletic commitments, and a recognition of the mental and physical toll that athletics can take. Proactive academic planning is crucial, ensuring that athletes are not only meeting the NCAA's academic standards but are also on a path that accommodates their sports schedules and promotes long-term academic and career success. With a holistic approach to understanding the student-athlete, colleges and universities can foster an environment where athletic and academic pursuits are not in competition, but rather complementary elements of a well-rounded collegiate experience.

Components of Academic Support Programs

Academic support programs for student-athletes typically include a combination of academic advising, tutoring services, study halls, and life skills development. These programs aim to enhance academic performance, improve time management, and foster person and professional development.

Enhancing Academic Performance

Enhancing academic performance for student-athletes requires a tailored approach that accommodates their unique demands and schedules. Personalized advising plays a pivotal role in this endeavor, offering a structured academic roadmap that aligns with their sporting commitments. Advisors work closely with student-athletes to select courses that fit into their rigorous training schedules, ensure compliance with NCAA academic standards, and provide strategies for academic success. By receiving personalized guidance, student-athletes can navigate their coursework more effectively, avoiding potential scheduling conflicts and academic pitfalls. Tutoring services supplement this personalized advising by providing targeted academic support in challenging subjects. With access to subject-specific tutors who understand the pressures of athletic schedules, student-athletes can receive the help they need to grasp complex concepts, complete assignments, and prepare for exams outside traditional classroom hours.

This comprehensive support system is designed not just for maintaining eligibility but also for ensuring that student-athletes make consistent progress toward their degrees. Academic advisors and tutors collaborate to create an environment that fosters learning and intellectual growth, acknowledging that each student-athlete has individual strengths and areas for improvement. By focusing on both immediate and long-term academic goals, these services help student-athletes to stay on track for graduation, ensuring that their education remains a priority alongside their athletic endeavors. Moreover, by addressing academic challenges early and providing ongoing support, institutions can help student-athletes to build the confidence and skills necessary for academic achievement, setting a foundation for success that extends beyond their collegiate sports careers.

Time Management Skills

Improving time management is a vital skill for student-athletes, who must often synchronize the rigorous demands of athletic training with academic responsibilities. To assist them, many institutions offer workshops and individual counseling sessions that focus on developing effective time management strategies. These educational interventions are designed to equip student-athletes with the tools they need to organize their schedules efficiently, prioritize tasks, and maximize productivity. By breaking down their daily routines into manageable segments, student-athletes can allocate adequate time for class attendance, study sessions, team practices, and competitive events, as well as crucial downtime for rest and personal activities.

Individual counseling sessions provide a tailored approach to time management, addressing each student-athlete's specific circumstances. Counselors can help athletes create personalized schedules that reflect their academic deadlines and athletic timetables, ensuring they meet both educational and training goals. They can also teach techniques for avoiding procrastination, managing stress, and staying organized—a trifecta of skills that can significantly impact an athlete's ability to balance their dual roles. By fostering these time management capabilities, student-athletes can improve their academic performance, enhance their athletic development, and ultimately enjoy a more harmonious and less stressful college experience.

Personal and Professional Development

Fostering personal and professional development in student-athletes is an investment in their future that goes well beyond their time on the field or court. Life skills workshops are integral components of this developmental arc, addressing crucial areas such as financial literacy, leadership, communication, and career planning. These workshops aim to prepare student-athletes for the complexities and challenges of life after college sports, equipping them with the knowledge to manage finances effectively, communicate clearly, lead with confidence, and make informed decisions about their career paths. By introducing these subjects early in their college journey, student-athletes can begin to cultivate a vision for their post-athletic career and personal life that is both realistic and ambitious.

Moreover, workshops on leadership and communication not only serve student-athletes in hypothetical future scenarios but also in their current roles within their teams and academic settings. The skills learned are directly applicable to teamwork, group projects, and networking opportunities. Similarly, financial literacy training provides them with the know-how to manage any earnings from part-time jobs or future salaries wisely, an essential skill given that many student-athletes will not go on to professional sports careers. In combining these life skills with career planning resources, institutions help ensure that student-athletes are as prepared for the next chapter of their lives as they are for the next game, fostering well-rounded individuals ready to make positive contributions to society.

The Transformative Power of a Scholarship

Many institutions have developed comprehensive academic support programs that have significantly contributed to the success of their student-athletes. For example, universities with high graduation rates among athletes often attribute this success to their academic support services, highlighting the value of these programs in promoting academic achievement and athlete well-being.

Athletic scholarships provide a crucial bridge for many student-athletes, enabling them to pursue higher education and compete at elite levels, despite the slim odds of turning professional in their sports. With the NCAA reporting that very few college athletes make it to the professional ranks, an often overlooked aspect of college sports is its role in fostering academic achievement, discipline, and financial security.

Balancing athletics with academic and social commitments is a formidable challenge, raising questions about the worth of such a demanding lifestyle for those unlikely to pursue sports professionally. However, many student-athletes note the profound benefits of collegiate athletics beyond the playing field. Research and experts alike tout the positive impact of being a student-athlete, from higher graduation rates and GPAs to the development of life skills such as teamwork, discipline, and time management.

Athletic scholarships emerge as a critical factor in this equation, offering financial security that is increasingly rare in an era of escalating college costs and student debt, which has neared the $1 trillion mark in the United States. These scholarships cover not just tuition, but often room, board, and other essentials, potentially saving student-athletes hundreds of thousands of dollars, an advantage that extends well beyond their college years into future financial stability.

The discipline required to juggle workouts, practices, classes, and study hours instills a work ethic and time management skills that serve student-athletes long after graduation. This regimen prepares them for the complexities of career and family life, giving them a competitive edge in the workforce. Indeed, the structure and demands of being a student-athlete can translate into successful careers, with employers valuing the traits honed on the field and in the classroom.

Moreover, the educational benefits are significant. NCAA requirements ensure that student-athletes maintain high academic standards, contributing to better school performance and potentially more lucrative career paths. Networking opportunities with fellow athletes and alumni further enhance their future prospects.

While the path of a student-athlete is undoubtedly challenging, requiring sacrifices and a relentless pursuit of excellence, the rewards—academic, personal, and professional—are immense. The opportunities afforded by athletic scholarships is a testament to the power of sports as a catalyst for positive change. A passion for athletics, combined with the support of institutions like the NCAA, opens doors to education, cultivates essential life skills, and paves the way for future success, both on and off the field.

Challenges and Considerations

Implementing effective academic support for student-athletes indeed presents a unique set of challenges that educational institutions must navigate. One of the most significant hurdles is securing adequate funding for comprehensive programs. With limited budgets and competing financial priorities, universities often struggle to allocate sufficient resources for academic advisors, tutors, and specialized learning workshops. This scarcity of funds can limit the availability and quality of support services provided, potentially impacting the academic success of student-athletes who require these resources the most.

Another challenge lies in overcoming the stigma associated with seeking academic help. In the competitive world of collegiate athletics, there is often an unwarranted perception that needing academic assistance equates to a lack of intelligence or effort. This stigma can deter student-athletes from taking advantage of academic support services, exacerbating the risk of academic underperformance. Changing this mindset requires a cultural shift within athletic departments to normalize and even encourage the utilization of academic resources as a part of a student-athlete's routine.

Furthermore, the task of customizing support to meet the diverse needs of student-athletes is intricate. Athletes from different sports disciplines follow varied training and competition schedules, which can conflict with academic responsibilities. Moreover, student-athletes represent a range of academic majors with distinct demands and workload intensities. Academic support services must be flexible and personalized to address these differences, providing an adaptable framework that can cater to the individual academic journey of each student-athlete.

Addressing these challenges is critical because the academic support of student-athletes underpins not just their educational attainment but their overall college experience. Such support ensures that the dual responsibilities of athletics and academics do not become an overwhelming burden. Instead, they should coalesce into a harmonious collegiate career that encourages growth in both arenas. Academic excellence and personal development are not mutually exclusive; with the right support, they are complementary goals that, when achieved, contribute to the holistic development of student-athletes.

While the journey to delivering effective academic support to student-athletes is fraught with challenges, the rewards are manifold. By fostering a culture that values academic excellence as much as athletic achievement, institutions lay the groundwork for their athletes to succeed not just in the stadium but in life beyond college sports. The considerations and efforts made to address these challenges will ultimately benefit not only the student-athletes themselves but the entire ethos of the institution, promoting a legacy of well-rounded excellence and integrity.

Discussion Questions

- How can institutions better support student-athletes in balancing their academic and athletic responsibilities?
- What are the key components of an effective academic support program tailored to the unique needs of student-athletes?
- How can academic support services for student-athletes be designed to also prepare them for life and careers after college sports?
- What are the most effective strategies to secure funding for academic support programs for student-athletes, and how can institutions ensure these resources are sustainably allocated?
- How can colleges and universities work to dismantle the stigma associated with student-athletes seeking academic help, and what role can coaches and fellow athletes play in this process?
- In what ways can academic support programs be personalized to cater to the varying schedules and academic needs of student-athletes across different sports?
- How do academic pressures affect the mental health of student-athletes, and what support systems can be put in place to address these issues proactively?
- What role does the NCAA play in the academic support of student-athletes, and are there policies that could be implemented to enhance the effectiveness of academic support programs?
- How can academic success be quantified and evaluated within athletic programs to ensure that student-athletes are making genuine progress?
- What collaborative efforts can be made between academic departments and athletic programs to create a seamless support system for student-athletes?

Case Study 13.1: Enhancing Academic Performance through Advising

At Oceanview University, the athletic department recognized that its student-athletes were consistently underperforming academically compared to the non-athlete student body. Analysis revealed that student-athletes struggled with core subjects, had lower GPAs, and a higher dropout rate. The university attributed these challenges to the lack of a structured academic support system that addressed the specific needs of student-athletes.

The Event
In response, Oceanview University launched a pilot program named the "Athlete Academic Advancement Initiative" (A3I), focusing on personalized academic advising and tutoring for student-athletes. A3I aimed to provide targeted support in difficult subjects, develop customized academic plans, and offer skills workshops. The advising team consisted of academic counselors with a background in sports education, who worked in close collaboration with coaches to ensure training schedules were synchronized with academic deadlines.

The Impact
The implementation of A3I led to a noticeable improvement in the academic performance of student-athletes. By the end of the first year, the average GPA of student-athletes increased by 0.5 points. The program also reported a 30% decrease in academic probation rates among athletes and a higher graduation rate compared to the years prior to the initiative. Furthermore, student-athletes reported feeling more confident in managing their academic responsibilities alongside their athletic commitments.

Discussion
- How can personalized advising be scaled to accommodate a larger number of student-athletes while maintaining the quality of support?
- What measures can be put in place to continuously assess and ensure the effectiveness of academic support programs like A3I?
- How can the relationship between academic advisors and athletic coaches be optimized to support student-athlete success?
- In what ways might the introduction of academic support initiatives like A3I influence the recruitment of future student-athletes?
- What long-term personal and professional development benefits can student-athletes gain from programs such as A3I?

Case Study 13.2: Time Management Through Workshop Interventions

Riverside College had a burgeoning sports program with teams increasingly excelling in regional and national competitions. However, academic advisors at Riverside noted a trend of student-athletes facing difficulties managing their time effectively, which affected their academic and athletic performances. The problem was particularly pronounced for teams with extensive travel schedules.

The Event

To address this, Riverside College initiated a "Time Mastery for Athletes" workshop series. The program included sessions on prioritizing tasks, utilizing planning tools, and strategies for optimizing travel and downtime for study. The workshops were designed to be interactive and sport-specific, recognizing the different demands placed on athletes from various sports. Attendance was integrated into the athletes' schedules as a mandatory element of their training program.

The Impact

The workshops proved to be highly effective, with student-athletes showing marked improvements in their ability to manage academic deadlines and reduce stress levels. Athletes also reported a better quality of life and improved performance in their sports as they were able to train more effectively. Riverside College saw a decline in last-minute withdrawal from classes and an increase in the timely submission of assignments. Moreover, the program's success led to its adoption as a regular offering for all incoming student-athletes during orientation.

Discussion

- How can the effectiveness of the "Time Mastery for Athletes" workshops be evaluated on a long-term basis?
- What role can technology play in further enhancing the time management skills of student-athletes?
- How can the experiences of upperclassmen who have benefited from the program be integrated into the workshops for peer mentoring?
- Should time management training be mandatory for all student-athletes, or should it be on an as-needed basis?
- What adjustments can be made to the workshops to accommodate the unique challenges faced by elite student-athletes who may have professional sports prospects?

Chapter 14
Broadcasting and Media Rights of Collegiate Athletics

Collegiate athletics operate within a unique nexus of educational institutions, sports, business, and media. This interplay has transformed over the years into a multi-billion-dollar enterprise, significantly shaping the landscape of higher education and sports entertainment. The broadcasting and media rights associated with collegiate sports are at the heart of this transformation. This chapter provides a comprehensive overview of these rights, discussing historical developments, current trends, and future implications.

Upon successful completion of this unit, students will be able to:

- Understand the historical evolution of broadcasting and media rights in collegiate athletics from their inception to present day.
- Identify the impact of the Supreme Court's 1984 NCAA v. Board of Regents decision on the distribution of television rights and revenue in collegiate sports.
- Recognize the role of collegiate athletic conferences in negotiating broadcasting contracts and how these agreements influence conference realignments and the establishment of network channels.
- Examine how digital media platforms have changed the broadcasting landscape of collegiate sports and their implications for fan engagement and content dissemination.
- Analyze the ethical and legal considerations surrounding the use of student-athletes' likenesses in media and broadcasting, including the debate on compensation.
- Anticipate future trends and challenges in the broadcasting and media rights arena of collegiate athletics, considering technological advancements and shifts in consumer habits.

Historical Context

In the early decades of the 20th century, the intersection of collegiate athletics and media was marked by a simplicity that belied the massive commercial enterprise it would become. Radio, with its capacity to carry the excitement of live sports into homes, became the first mass medium to broadcast college games, creating a new kind of communal experience around collegiate sports. However, it was the advent of television that truly transformed the sector, turning local and regional pastimes into national spectacles. The visual medium opened up the sports field beyond the stands, enabling fans to follow their beloved teams from the comfort of their living rooms. As television sets became a household staple, the demand for college sports content grew, laying the foundation for the broadcasting networks' future battles over airing rights.

The post-World War II era, especially, witnessed a boom in television ownership and with it, the growth of the collegiate sports audience. College football and basketball games, brimming with pageantry and passion, proved to be perfect fodder for the new medium. Networks, quick to capitalize on the burgeoning popularity, entered into fierce competition for the broadcasting rights of these collegiate contests. This competition was not merely for the prestige of association with collegiate athletics but for the substantial revenue from advertisers who recognized the value of the attentive audiences these sports attracted. The resulting bidding wars drove up the cost of broadcasting rights, funneling unprecedented revenue into collegiate athletic programs and laying the groundwork for the financial structure of modern college sports.

As the 20th century progressed, the relationship between collegiate athletics and broadcasting evolved into a symbiotic one, with each driving the growth of the other. Television turned local heroes into national stars and marquee matchups into national events, while the expanding reach of media broadcasts fueled the growth of fanbases and the commercial appeal of collegiate sports. Major games became prime-time events, and landmark matchups like the Rose Bowl and March Madness became cultural phenomena. The media rights attached to these games grew to be so valuable that they prompted regulatory and structural changes within the collegiate athletic associations themselves. This evolution set the stage for the complex, highly lucrative broadcasting landscape that underpins collegiate athletics today.

The NCAA and Broadcasting Rights

For much of its history, the NCAA maintained stringent control over the broadcasting rights of collegiate sports. This governing body, with its centralized command, was responsible for negotiating television contracts on behalf of its member institutions. These deals were made under the auspices of protecting the amateur status of athletes and ensuring the equitable distribution of resources among its membership. However, critics argued that the NCAA's stronghold on broadcasting stifled competition and innovation within collegiate sports media. The NCAA's policies meant that individual schools and conferences had little say in the negotiation process, often accepting terms set forth by the association without room for bargaining to their advantage.

The monopoly of the NCAA over broadcasting rights was challenged in the landmark antitrust lawsuit, NCAA v. Board of Regents of the University of Oklahoma, which reached the Supreme Court in 1984. The Court ruled that the NCAA's control over television contracts violated antitrust laws by restraining trade and limiting competition. This pivotal decision transformed the economic landscape of collegiate sports, dismantling the NCAA's tight rein over broadcasting rights and opening the door for free-market principles to enter the collegiate athletics broadcasting domain. The ruling recognized the rights of individual schools and conferences to negotiate their own television contracts, leading to a significant diversification of the collegiate sports broadcasting market.

In the wake of the Supreme Court's decision, a surge in revenue generation for collegiate athletics ensued, particularly for football and basketball programs. Conferences, now able to negotiate their own television deals, leveraged their most popular sports to secure lucrative contracts with major networks. Schools with strong football or basketball programs found themselves in a position to command higher fees, reflecting the market value of their sports' popularity. This shift not only led to an increase in the revenues generated from broadcasting rights but also catalyzed an era of substantial financial growth for many athletic programs. The newfound autonomy allowed conferences to innovate, leading to the creation of their own networks and exploring new avenues for content delivery, such as digital streaming, further expanding their reach and revenue potential.

The Role of Conferences

In the years following the pivotal 1984 Supreme Court ruling, collegiate athletic conferences quickly realized the power they held collectively and began to seize control of the burgeoning market for broadcast rights. Understanding the substantial value these rights held, conferences like the SEC, Big Ten, and Pac-12 started to aggressively negotiate contracts with major television networks. These deals were not merely transactional; they represented a strategic move to enhance the visibility and profitability of their member institutions. With each conference vying to maximize its media exposure and revenue streams, the collegiate sports broadcasting landscape underwent a significant transformation, one where conferences emerged not just as academic alliances, but as influential media entities in their own right.

This shift in control also catalyzed changes in the traditional collegiate athletic alignments as schools began to place greater emphasis on television marketability. As a result, conference realignment became a strategic game, with schools moving in and out of conferences based not only on geographic proximity and competitive balance, but also on their potential to attract lucrative television deals. The realignment dance also led to the development of conference-specific networks, like the Big Ten Network, which became platforms for showcasing events and programming tailored to their respective audiences. These networks generated additional revenue for member schools and further solidified the power conferences held in the national sports dialogue.

The Current Landscape

The contemporary broadcasting and media rights landscape of collegiate athletics is a high-stakes, high-reward environment dominated by large-scale contracts and intense bidding wars among major networks and streaming services. Marquee events such as the College Football Playoff and the NCAA Men's Basketball Tournament are hot commodities, securing deals that generate staggering revenue streams for participating schools and conferences. These agreements are vital to the financial well-being of athletic departments, as they often provide the means to fund an array of sports programs, including those that do not generate significant revenue on their own. This influx of capital has not only elevated the production quality of broadcasts but also reinforced the commercial importance of collegiate sports within the broader entertainment industry.

The proliferation of digital media has further transformed the broadcasting rights paradigm. Streaming services have become formidable contenders in acquiring broadcasting rights, offering live game coverage, and producing a wealth of original programming tailored to the collegiate sports market. This shift has democratized content access, enabling fans to watch games and engage with their favorite teams across an array of devices, regardless of their geographical location. The integration of social media platforms, offering real-time highlights and fan interaction, has added layers of connectivity and fan engagement, bolstering the reach and influence of collegiate sports.

As the media landscape continues to evolve with advancements in technology and changes in consumer behavior, the strategic importance of digital platforms in collegiate sports broadcasting is poised for further growth. The competition among traditional networks is now compounded by the rise of tech companies with deep pockets and a willingness to invest in live sports content. This convergence of technology, media, and collegiate athletics heralds a new era where the rules of engagement are being rewritten, promising innovative viewing experiences and further amplification of the collegiate athletics brand.

The current broadcasting rights landscape in collegiate athletics reflects a dynamic and complex interplay of traditional broadcasting, digital innovation, and evolving fan expectations. As stakeholders navigate this terrain, the enduring challenge remains balancing the commercial imperatives of media rights deals with the educational and developmental mission of collegiate athletics. How this balance is struck will undoubtedly shape the future trajectory of college sports broadcasting.

Ethical and Legal Considerations

The surge in broadcasting revenues from collegiate athletics has ignited a debate on the ethical treatment and legal rights of student-athletes, particularly around the concept of amateurism that underpins college sports. While institutions and athletic programs benefit financially from lucrative media deals, the athletes themselves, whose performances are central to these broadcasts, have historically not received compensation commensurate with their contribution. This discrepancy has spurred a discourse on the fairness of profit distribution within collegiate sports, challenging the traditional amateur model that prohibits student-athletes from receiving a share of the revenue generated from the use of their name, image, and likeness.

Legal challenges have arisen as a response to this growing tension, most notably in the case of O'Bannon v. NCAA, where the NCAA's practices of profiting from the likenesses of its athletes without providing them compensation were put under judicial scrutiny. The ruling in favor of O'Bannon signaled a significant shift, as courts began to question the legality of the NCAA's amateurism rules under antitrust laws. The O'Bannon case has paved the way for further legal inquiries and has pressured the NCAA to reconsider its policies, leading to incremental reforms that hint at a future where athletes could potentially negotiate their own rights within the collegiate sports market.

The ongoing ethical and legal conversation surrounding broadcasting rights and athlete compensation reflects a broader societal questioning of equity and labor rights within the commercialized realm of college sports. These discussions extend beyond the courtrooms and conference tables, engaging the public, academia, and policymakers in a critical examination of what constitutes fair play in the business of sports. As the landscape evolves, with potential legislative actions and further court decisions, the collegiate athletics community may witness transformative changes in how broadcasting rights are managed and how student-athletes are recognized and rewarded for their roles in this lucrative industry.

The Impact on Academic Institutions

The windfall from media rights in collegiate athletics has dramatically altered the financial dynamics of academic institutions, creating both opportunities and challenges. The substantial revenue from broadcast contracts has empowered universities to enhance their athletic departments, funding state-of-the-art facilities, and expanding athletic staff, which in turn can elevate the institution's profile and attractiveness to prospective students. However, this influx of funds has stirred a debate over the prioritization of resources within educational settings. Critics argue that the disproportionate emphasis on athletic success, driven in part by media visibility and revenue, may skew an institution's allocation of resources away from academic departments and educational endeavors, raising questions about the core mission of these institutions.

The nexus between revenue-driven athletics and academic integrity has also placed student-athlete welfare under scrutiny. With the rigorous demands of media engagements, coupled with the pressure to perform athletically, student-athletes can find themselves in a challenging balancing act, striving to meet the expectations of their sports commitments while also fulfilling academic responsibilities. Furthermore, the broadcasting spotlight can intensify the scrutiny and pressure on these young athletes, impacting their mental health and academic performance. As such, the need for policies that safeguard the educational experience and well-being of student-athletes against the backdrop of a profit-oriented sports media environment has become more pronounced.

The debate around the impact of media rights revenue on academic institutions is a microcosm of the broader dialogue on the commercialization of higher education. As the landscape of collegiate sports continues to be shaped by broadcasting deals, it remains imperative for academic institutions to navigate these complexities thoughtfully. Ensuring that the infusion of media rights revenue serves the broader educational mission, while maintaining equity and supporting the holistic development of student-athletes, is an ongoing challenge that requires careful consideration and strategic planning by university leaders and stakeholders.

The Future of Broadcasting and Media Rights

The future of broadcasting and media rights in collegiate athletics appears poised for continued growth and evolution, driven by technological innovation and shifting consumer behaviors. As audiences increasingly turn to digital and on-demand media consumption, rights holders and collegiate athletic programs must adapt, exploring new platforms and formats to deliver content. The potential expansion of the College Football Playoff, for instance, offers an opportunity to leverage the increased number of games for broader distribution and greater revenue generation. Additionally, the conversations surrounding athlete compensation, fueled by state laws and changing NCAA policies, suggest that the structure of media rights deals could be reexamined to potentially include revenue-sharing models with student-athletes.

The rise of new media platforms, including social media and direct-to-consumer streaming services, signals a shift in how collegiate sports are packaged and consumed. This digital transformation opens the door for institutions to cultivate direct relationships with their fan bases, bypassing traditional broadcast methods. Moreover, the proliferation of high-speed internet and mobile devices is likely to democratize content distribution, allowing for more personalized and interactive viewer experiences. Consequently, future negotiations and the allocation of media rights revenue will have to consider the value added by enhanced viewer engagement and data analytics that these digital platforms provide.

In this rapidly changing landscape, those involved in collegiate athletics administration must have a robust understanding of the intricacies of media rights and their implications for the future of college sports. The decisions made today will resonate for years to come, potentially altering the very nature of collegiate athletics. As administrators grapple with these complex issues, they must balance commercial interests with the educational and developmental mission of their institutions, ensuring that the spirit of competition and sportsmanship remains at the heart of collegiate athletics.

Discussion Questions

- How has the Supreme Court's 1984 decision in NCAA v. Board of Regents of the University of Oklahoma fundamentally changed the business model of collegiate sports broadcasting?
- In what ways have collegiate athletic conferences benefited from negotiating their own media rights deals, and what has been the impact on the smaller, less marketable programs?
- How do the massive broadcasting contracts for events like the College Football Playoff and March Madness reconcile with the NCAA's stance on maintaining amateurism in college sports?
- Discuss the ethical implications of the commercialization of collegiate athletics through media rights, especially in relation to the ongoing debate over student-athlete compensation.
- How has the rise of digital streaming platforms affected the traditional broadcasting model for collegiate sports, and what could this mean for future media rights negotiations?
- How might advancements in technology and changes in consumer media consumption influence the strategy behind broadcasting and media rights for collegiate sports in the next decade?
- In light of recent discussions about athlete compensation, what are some viable models that could be implemented to ensure fair compensation for student-athletes while maintaining the integrity of collegiate sports?

Case Study 14.1: The Realignment of Conferences and Media Rights

Collegiate sports in the United States have traditionally been grouped into conferences based on geographical and institutional affiliations. These conferences not only organize athletic competition schedules but also play a crucial role in negotiating media rights for their member institutions. In the past decade, several high-profile realignments of colleges and universities among conferences have occurred, altering the traditional landscape of collegiate athletics.

The Event
One of the most notable realignments involved the Big Ten Conference, which, in pursuit of expanding its television market, added the University of Maryland and Rutgers University as its newest members in 2014. These institutions were previously part of the Atlantic Coast Conference (ACC) and the Big East Conference, respectively. This strategic move was influenced by the potential to access the lucrative New York and Washington D.C. media markets, thereby increasing the value of the Big Ten's media rights and providing greater revenue opportunities for all members through the Big Ten Network.

The Impact

The inclusion of Maryland and Rutgers expanded the Big Ten's geographical footprint and viewer base. This not only provided the conference with enhanced bargaining power in television rights negotiations but also led to a significant increase in revenue from its broadcasting deals. For Maryland and Rutgers, the shift meant greater financial stability and visibility for their athletic programs. However, it also sparked concerns about increased travel costs, the loss of traditional rivalries, and the impact on student-athlete welfare due to longer distances for away competitions.

Discussion

- How do conference realignments, driven by the pursuit of media rights revenue, align with the mission of collegiate athletics and higher education institutions?
- What are the potential long-term consequences for athletic programs that shift conferences in terms of fan engagement and historical rivalries?
- How do the benefits of increased media rights revenue weigh against the potential downsides, such as the disruption of traditional conference alignments and increased demands on student-athletes?
- Should the NCAA have a more active role in overseeing conference realignments to ensure alignment with the broader educational goals of student-athlete development?

Case Study 14.2: Impact of Streaming on NCAA Broadcasting Rights

The rise of streaming services has significantly impacted the broadcasting landscape across various entertainment sectors, with collegiate athletics being no exception. These platforms offer an alternative to traditional broadcasting methods, attracting a younger, tech-savvy demographic that increasingly prefers on-demand and mobile access to content.

The Event

In a groundbreaking deal, a prominent streaming service secured the rights to stream several major collegiate basketball and football games, including exclusive coverage of select postseason matchups. This deal marked a shift from traditional network broadcasting to a more digital-centric approach, catering to the changing consumption habits of sports fans. The streaming service implemented interactive features, such as in-game statistics and social media integration, enhancing the viewer experience.

The Impact

The introduction of streaming services to the collegiate sports broadcasting rights mix has had several significant impacts. It opened up new revenue streams for collegiate athletic departments and conferences, diversified the ways in which fans could engage with content, and set a precedent for future negotiations of media rights. However, it also raised concerns about market segmentation and the potential for reduced audience reach for those without access to streaming technology. Institutions had to navigate these changes while maintaining equitable exposure for all sports programs.

Discussion

- How might the introduction of streaming services alter the existing dynamics of media rights distribution among collegiate athletic programs?
- What are the implications for accessibility and inclusivity as collegiate sports broadcasting moves towards a digital-first model?
- In what ways can collegiate athletic departments leverage streaming technology to enhance fan engagement and create new experiences for viewers?
- How can institutions balance the financial benefits of exclusive streaming deals with the potential risk of alienating fans who rely on traditional broadcast methods?

Chapter 15
Globalization of College Sports

The landscape of college sports is undergoing a transformative shift, reflecting the broader trends of globalization evident in various sectors worldwide. This chapter delves into the expanding international interest in college sports, which has traditionally been viewed as a predominantly North American phenomenon. It also explores the growing trend of international athletes choosing to participate in the American college sports system, a move that contrasts with their earlier inclination to remain within the international club sports system.

Upon successful completion of this chapter, students will be able to:

- Identify the digital platforms and technologies that have contributed to the international broadcasting of college sports.
- Explain how social media facilitates the creation of global fan communities and engages international audiences.
- Evaluate the benefits and challenges associated with offering scholarships to international students.
- Discuss the contributions of international athletes to team dynamics, performance, and cultural diversity.
- Identify the challenges faced by international athletes in adapting to the American college sports environment and the support systems available to assist them.
- Critically analyze the ethical implications of recruiting international athletes, including the impact on domestic athletes and the potential for exploitation.
- Predict the potential future trends in the globalization of college sports, including international collaborations and the development of global sports academies.
- Formulate strategies for colleges and universities to leverage the globalization of college sports while ensuring fairness and inclusivity.

The Global Audience for College Sports

College sports, particularly in the United States, have cultivated a unique global audience, transcending borders and connecting diverse cultures through the universal language of competition and athletic excellence. This international interest is spurred not only by the high level of play and the vibrant, pageantry-filled atmospheres of college games but also by the increasing number of international athletes who choose to compete in the NCAA, bringing with them a loyal following from their home countries. Platforms like social media, international broadcasting agreements, and online streaming services have further diminished geographical barriers, allowing fans around the world to follow their favorite teams and athletes in real-time. This global engagement not only enriches the college sports experience, offering a broader perspective and heightened competition, but also underscores sports' powerful role in fostering international camaraderie and cultural exchange.

Expanding International Broadcasts and Streaming

The digital age has revolutionized the consumption of college sports, turning it into a global phenomenon. With live streaming services and platforms burgeoning, fans from all corners of the world now have the means to watch games and tournaments in real-time, breaking free from the constraints that once limited viewership to the geographic boundaries of North America. This technological leap has transformed the way fans interact with their favorite college sports, allowing them to follow their preferred teams and athletes with an immediacy that was previously unimaginable. This evolution in broadcast technology not only democratizes access to college sports but also serves as a bridge between disparate cultures, fostering a global community of sports enthusiasts.

The implications of this global reach extend far beyond mere viewership. For international fans, the ability to stream live events and access comprehensive coverage means a deeper, more nuanced understanding and appreciation of the games. It empowers fans to engage with the sports narrative, the seasonal highs and lows, and the personal journeys of the athletes, thereby cultivating a more invested and informed fan base. Furthermore, the proliferation of digital platforms offers colleges and sports programs a lucrative opportunity to tap into international markets, effectively increasing their brand visibility and, by extension, opening up new revenue streams through advertising and merchandising. These platforms also provide an interactive space where fans can engage with each other and share their passion, creating vibrant online communities that act as focal points for fan interaction and engagement on a global scale.

However, the shift toward digital streaming and international broadcasting of college sports also raises questions about the long-term implications for fan engagement. As audiences grow more diverse, the demand for tailored content that addresses the specific interests and cultural nuances of a global audience becomes paramount. This requires broadcasters and platforms to adopt more inclusive and multifaceted strategies to maintain and expand their international viewership. Consequently, colleges and sports programs must consider multilingual services, culturally sensitive content creation, and timing broadcasts to suit different time zones. In doing so, they not only enrich the viewing experience for international fans but also foster a sense of community and belonging among a diverse audience, strengthening global connections through the shared language of sports.

Social Media and International Fan Bases

The infiltration of social media into the realm of college sports has catalyzed the formation of robust international fan bases. Platforms like Twitter, Facebook, Instagram, and TikTok have become instrumental in transcending physical distances, allowing fans from various parts of the globe to rally around their favorite college teams and athletes. Colleges and athletic programs harness these platforms to publish updates, game highlights, behind-the-scenes footage, and athlete stories, which resonate with and engage an international audience. By curating content that reflects the diverse interests of this wide audience, these institutions foster a sense of inclusivity and community. The potential for real-time interaction on these platforms further enhances the connection between international fans and the teams they support, creating a dynamic and interactive fan experience that keeps the global audience engaged across different time zones and languages.

To cater to an international audience, colleges and athletic programs are increasingly producing multilingual content. Recognizing the diverse linguistic background of their international fans, they offer key updates, articles, and video content in multiple languages. This not only broadens their reach but also shows a commitment to inclusivity, acknowledging and valuing the global fan base's diversity. Moreover, the use of subtitles and closed captions on video content ensures that language barriers do not hinder the enjoyment of the sport. By making their content accessible in this way, colleges are able to nurture a closer relationship with their international followers, who in turn feel seen and heard.

Collaborations with international sports influencers offer another strategic avenue for expanding the reach of college sports. Influencers with substantial followings can act as bridges, introducing new audiences to college sports and providing relatable commentary that resonates with cultural nuances. These collaborations can take various forms, from influencers attending games and sharing their experiences to them participating in campaigns that highlight the values and traditions of college sports. Athletic programs can leverage these influencers' insights to tailor their outreach strategies, tapping into the local knowledge that these influencers possess about what engages fans in their respective regions. Through such strategic partnerships, colleges can authentically engage with international fans, fostering a passionate and loyal following that spans continents.

International Athletes in College Sports

International student-athletes (ISAs) are a distinct and significant group within the United States collegiate system. Combining the roles of international students and NCAA athletes, they face a complex adjustment process upon arrival. This process is more demanding than that faced by domestic students, requiring navigation through academic rigors, athletic commitments, and cultural acclimatization. While ISAs often possess strong educational backgrounds, reflecting rigorous selection criteria for international admissions, they paradoxically experience higher dropout rates compared to domestic student-athletes (DSAs). This suggests that the challenges ISAs encounter extend well beyond academics, impacting their ability to integrate socially and adjust to a new cultural environment.

The cultural and social adaptation for ISAs can be particularly strenuous. They must grapple with the nuances of a new social landscape, language barriers, and in some cases, racial discrimination. These factors are not merely peripheral but central to their well-being and success, as they can greatly affect both mental health and performance in sports and academics. Furthermore, ISAs often view their athletic participation differently from DSAs, seeing it not as the pinnacle of their college experience but as part of a broader educational journey. This outlook shapes their engagement with sports, expectations from their collegiate athletic experience, and overall performance.

Recruitment and institutional choice for ISAs are compounded by the logistical limitations they face, such as the inability to visit U.S. campuses. Consequently, their decisions may hinge more on athletic scholarship offers and the perceived quality of interactions with coaching staff, rather than a well-rounded understanding of the institution's academic and cultural fit. In addition to recruitment challenges, ISAs must contend with the NCAA's stringent eligibility criteria, which often clash with varying global standards of amateurism. The rigorous investigation into their past involvement with professional sports, which may differ from U.S. practices, leads to a disproportionate number of eligibility issues among ISAs.

Socioeconomic status and gender further influence the ISA experience. The capacity to finance their education in the U.S., the interplay of gender norms within sports, and how cultural identity intersects with socioeconomic background all shape their journey. Women ISAs, in particular, may face additional gender-related barriers within the sports domain and broader societal expectations. Addressing these multifaceted challenges calls for comprehensive support systems sensitive to the unique needs of ISAs. Academic assistance that acknowledges language and educational differences, cultural sensitivity initiatives, mental health resources attuned to cultural and linguistic diversity, and an equitable NCAA eligibility assessment process are imperative.

The complex ISA experience mandates a multifaceted support strategy by educational institutions. It is essential to foster cross-departmental collaboration among academic advisors, athletic departments, international student services, and mental health professionals. By embracing a holistic approach that appreciates the varied backgrounds and requirements of ISAs, institutions can create a nurturing environment where these student-athletes can flourish academically, athletically, and in their personal lives. The success of ISAs hinges on the institution's commitment to providing tailored support and recognizing the diverse tapestry of experiences they bring to the collegiate athletic and academic arenas.

Why Recruit Internationally?

The infusion of international talent into NCAA sports is a growing trend driven by several compelling factors. Firstly, the globalization of sports has shattered geographical barriers, enabling NCAA coaches to tap into a global talent pool like never before. Advances in technology and communication, such as live streaming and social media, have played a pivotal role in this transformation. Coaches can now easily discover and monitor international talent through various channels and platforms. Moreover, sports tournaments and showcases held worldwide serve as magnets, attracting NCAA scouts to a rich diversity of players. This global expansion has effectively made the recruiting process borderless, opening up a wealth of opportunities for both athletes and coaches.

Another significant driver is the competitive advantage that international athletes can provide to NCAA teams. Athletes from different parts of the world often bring varied playing styles, techniques, and strategic thinking to their respective sports, which can be a game-changer for NCAA programs. For instance, European basketball players are renowned for their strong fundamentals, while soccer players from Latin America and Africa may introduce novel tactical nuances. This blend of styles and strategies enriches the team's play, posing a challenge for opponents to anticipate and counter. Such a competitive edge is invaluable in the NCAA landscape, where every team is looking to gain the upper hand.

Beyond the athletic benefits, international athletes also contribute to the academic and cultural fabric of college campuses. They embody the principles of diversity and inclusion, bringing new cultural perspectives and experiences into the classroom and the wider university community. This aligns with the mission of many institutions to foster a global learning environment and prepare students for a world that is increasingly interconnected. In the realm of sports, international athletes can help fill gaps in less popular programs or in positions that are traditionally harder to staff with domestic talent, offering flexibility in scholarship distribution and team dynamics. Success stories of international athletes in the NCAA further amplify the trend, serving as both inspiration and a powerful advertisement for the programs they represent.

The internationalization of NCAA sports rosters is not just a reflection of changing times; it's a strategic move that brings a wealth of benefits to both the athletes and the institutions they join. As NCAA sports continue to embrace athletes from across the globe, the athletic, academic, and cultural landscapes of colleges and universities are enriched, creating a dynamic environment where diverse talents and perspectives thrive.

The Future of Globalization in College Sports

The future of globalization in college sports is poised to chart a dynamic and integrative course, as institutions increasingly recognize the value of diverse talent pools and the benefits of cross-cultural exchanges. Enhanced recruitment strategies, bolstered by digital technology, are likely to further dissolve international borders, drawing a new wave of skilled athletes to NCAA programs. Collaborative efforts between colleges, sports federations, and international bodies may give rise to innovative training and development programs, thereby nurturing a generation of student-athletes equipped to excel both on the global stage and in their academic pursuits. With a commitment to inclusivity, equitable opportunities, and the holistic development of its international athletes, the NCAA can steer college sports into an era marked by worldwide engagement and enriched educational experiences.

Strategic Implications for Colleges and Universities

As the globalization of college sports accelerates, colleges and universities are at a strategic crossroads that necessitates forward-thinking approaches to maintain and enhance their competitive edge. The development of international collaborations is one such strategy, where institutions can forge partnerships with foreign educational and sports organizations. These alliances could offer dual benefits: providing a pathway for international talent to U.S. colleges, while also allowing domestic student-athletes to gain exposure and experience abroad. Furthermore, the creation of global sports academies affiliated with colleges could serve as feeder systems, identifying and nurturing young talent while providing a steady stream of well-prepared athletes to collegiate programs. These initiatives would not only boost the athletic prowess of college teams but also contribute to the cultural diversity and international profile of the institutions.

Moreover, bolstering international alumni networks is a strategic imperative for colleges seeking to sustain long-term global engagement in sports. Robust alumni networks can act as ambassadors of the institution's brand, opening doors for recruitment and fostering goodwill that can translate into future support, whether financial or logistical. Enhanced alumni relations can also facilitate mentorship opportunities, where past international student-athletes guide current ones, providing advice and helping them navigate the challenges of balancing academics with high-level competition. Additionally, alumni success stories can be powerful marketing tools that attract prospective athletes from across the globe. In harnessing the strength of these networks, colleges and universities can expand their global reach, ensure the well-being of their international athletes, and solidify their position in an increasingly interconnected collegiate sports landscape.

Ethical Considerations

The globalization of college sports, while opening doors to myriad opportunities, brings with it an array of ethical considerations that institutions must navigate with due diligence. One of the paramount concerns is ensuring equitable treatment for international athletes who join the ranks of NCAA sports teams. This not only includes fairness in recruitment and scholarship offerings but also in the ongoing support and resources provided to these students once they are part of the collegiate community. International athletes may face barriers such as language difficulties, cultural acclimatization, and potential isolation, which can impact their experience and success. Ensuring that these athletes receive the same level of care, attention, and opportunity as domestic athletes is a complex yet critical task, requiring thoughtful policies and intentional practices.

Moreover, the incorporation of international athletes into college sports programs must be examined for its impact on domestic athletes and programs. As resources are finite, the recruitment of international talent can lead to concerns about reduced opportunities for local athletes, shifts in team dynamics, and even changes in the culture of the sports programs themselves. It is imperative for institutions to strike a balance that upholds the spirit of inclusivity, fostering an environment where both international and domestic student-athletes can thrive. This balance is not only a matter of ethical responsibility but also a strategic imperative to maintain a harmonious and unified team ethos that is crucial for the success of any athletic program.

Lastly, the commitment to fairness and inclusivity extends to the broader implications of global recruitment on the NCAA sports landscape. This includes considering how the drive for a diverse roster aligns with the institution's mission and values, as well as the potential impact on the integrity of sports competitions. It also raises questions about the extent to which global aspirations should influence the core educational objectives of collegiate institutions. In this regard, reflection and ongoing dialogue are necessary to develop a framework that respects the rights and aspirations of all student-athletes, while fostering an equitable and respectful global sporting community. It is only through such ethical reflection that the true potential of globalization in college sports can be realized, benefiting not just the athletes but the entire spectrum of stakeholders involved.

Discussion Questions

- How can colleges and universities foster a more inclusive environment for international athletes?
- In what ways can the recruitment of international athletes be improved to ensure ethical practices and equitable opportunities?
- How do cultural differences impact the expectations and experiences of international athletes in NCAA sports, and what measures can be taken to foster an inclusive environment that respects these differences?
- How might the integration of ISAs influence team cohesion and dynamics, and what strategies can coaches and staff employ to facilitate positive interactions among diverse team members?
- In terms of financial support and scholarship allocation, how can institutions ethically manage the differing expectations and needs of international athletes compared to their domestic counterparts?

- How should colleges address the potential language barriers and educational challenges that international athletes may face, and what role do language support programs play in this context?
- What responsibilities do institutions have in supporting the mental health of international athletes, considering the unique stressors they may experience, and what specialized resources should be provided?
- What is the role of NCAA governance in managing the potential academic and athletic disparities that may arise from the recruitment of international athletes with varied backgrounds and levels of preparedness?

Case Study 15.1: Triumphs and Trials of an ISA

Elena Vasquez's journey to becoming a standout player on the University of Victory's women's basketball team began in her hometown of Madrid, Spain. With a passion for basketball ignited by her father, a former professional player, Elena quickly rose to prominence in Spain's competitive youth leagues. Her exceptional skills caught the eye of a Northern University scout during an international tournament.

The Event
Elena's recruitment was a blend of excitement and uncertainty. Northern University, seeking to bolster its women's basketball program with unique talent, embarked on the intensive recruitment of Elena, navigating complex NCAA eligibility requirements and leveraging digital communication to bridge the transatlantic gap. Despite cultural and language barriers, Elena's determination to excel both academically and athletically shone through, culminating in her acceptance of a scholarship offer.

The Impact
Elena's arrival in the U.S. was met with high expectations, and she did not disappoint. Her versatile playing style brought a new dynamism to the team, which contributed to a successful season that far exceeded previous years' performances. Off the court, Elena faced challenges adjusting to a new academic system and culture but found support through the university's international student programs. Her presence enriched the campus's cultural diversity and inspired other international students to consider collegiate sports in the U.S.

Discussion
- How can universities streamline the recruitment process for international athletes to ensure compliance and ease the transition?
- What specific resources can athletic programs provide to support the academic success of international student-athletes?

- In what ways do international athletes like Elena contribute to the diversity and competitiveness of college sports teams?
- How can colleges foster an inclusive environment that embraces the cultural contributions of international athletes?

Case Study 15.2: Innovative Strategies in Supporting ISAs

In an increasingly globalized world, college sports programs in the United States are extending their reach beyond national borders, seeking to attract top talent from around the globe. One such program, the State University Basketball Team (SUBT), recognized the untapped potential in diversifying its roster with international players. Understanding the mutual benefits, SUBT embarked on developing innovative recruitment and support strategies that align with their commitment to inclusivity and athletic excellence.

The Event
SUBT's athletic department launched a multifaceted initiative to bolster its international recruitment efforts. It established partnerships with basketball academies across Europe, Africa, and Asia, creating pipelines for talent scouting and cultural exchange. Additionally, the program hosted international basketball camps and participated in global tournaments, fostering direct engagement with potential recruits. Recognizing the challenges international athletes face, SUBT introduced a comprehensive support system that included language assistance, cultural integration programs, and a dedicated team liaison to help athletes navigate academic and athletic life.

The Impact
The innovative approach led to a significant rise in the number of international athletes at SUBT, with the basketball team showcasing players from six different countries within two seasons. This diversity brought a richness to the team's play style and spurred its success in national competitions. The academic performance and personal development of the international athletes also saw notable improvement, thanks to the robust support provided. The program's efforts did not go unnoticed, with SUBT earning a reputation as a leader in international student-athlete integration, enhancing its attractiveness to recruits worldwide.

Discussion
- How can college sports programs ensure that their international recruitment strategies are both ethical and effective?
- What role does cultural competency play in the success of international athletes, and how can programs foster an environment

that promotes this?
- In what ways do international athletes change the dynamics of college sports teams, and what strategies should coaches employ to harness these changes positively?
- What measures can institutions take to balance the athletic and academic needs of international athletes with those of domestic players?

Chapter 16
Sport Communication in Collegiate Athletics

In collegiate athletics, sport communication serves as a critical bridge connecting the activities on the field with various stakeholders such as the media, fans, athletes, and the institution itself. This chapter delves into the multifaceted nature of sport communication within the collegiate athletic landscape, focusing on its significance, strategies, and execution within the context of intercollegiate sports.

Upon successful completion of this unit, students will be able to:

- Identify the key components of effective sport communication within collegiate athletics and their impact on various stakeholders.
- Describe the strategies and best practices for managing media relations and generating positive publicity for athletic programs.
- Explain the role of digital media in enhancing fan engagement and building community around collegiate sports.
- Understand the principles of crisis communication and the preparation necessary to address potential issues in collegiate athletics effectively.
- Recognize the importance of compliance within sport communication and the collaborative relationship between compliance officers and communication professionals.
- Assess the influence of internal communication on organizational culture and its significance in maintaining a cohesive athletic department.

Foundations of Sport Communication

The foundations of sport communication within collegiate athletics form a pivotal aspect of how athletic departments interact with their internal and external environments. This intricate web of interaction involves crafting messages that not only resonate with the institution's mission and values but also serve to amplify the achievements of student-athletes and the successes of sports programs. To be effective, communication strategies need to be thoughtfully aligned with the institution's educational priorities, ensuring that the promotion of sports does not overshadow the academic purpose of the institution. Instead, it should foster a supportive culture that celebrates the dual roles of student-athletes as both competitors and scholars.

Public relations and media relations play a central role in the sphere of sport communication, acting as the conduit through which the institution's narrative is conveyed to the public. This narrative management includes not just the celebratory news of victories and individual accolades but also the educational and personal development opportunities provided through sports. The media is a crucial partner in this endeavor, serving as the platform for stories that can inspire, inform, and engage various audiences. Whether through press releases, interviews, or feature stories, a strong relationship with the media can help athletic departments navigate the balance between visibility and the sensitivity sometimes required in reporting.

Moreover, the realm of sport communication extends into the crucial territory of crisis communication and digital media management. Crisis communication demands preparedness and the capacity to respond swiftly and effectively to potential controversies or emergencies, safeguarding the reputation of the institution. Digital media management has become increasingly significant with the rise of social media as a primary means of interaction with fans and the community. It provides a unique space for real-time updates and engagement, requiring athletic departments to be both proactive and reactive in their digital strategies. To maintain the trust and support of the community, these communications must be handled with transparency, responsibility, and a focus on maintaining the integrity of the athletic programs and the institution at large.

Media Relations and Publicity

In the arena of collegiate athletics, media relations and publicity are essential for crafting the public persona of both the sports programs and the athletes. The athletic department's relationship with the media is cultivated through a combination of proactive outreach and responsive communication strategies. Proactive efforts such as issuing press releases, hosting media days, and organizing press conferences serve not only to celebrate successes and milestones but also to ensure that the narrative remains focused and favorable. These channels provide opportunities for institutions to spotlight the achievements of their teams and the exemplary accomplishments of student-athletes, from academic honors to community service involvement. By providing journalists with timely and accurate information, athletic departments can forge strong partnerships with media outlets, thereby facilitating fair and balanced reporting that benefits the institution's image and outreach.

Managing the media presence at events is another critical component of media relations. This involves more than just handling logistics; it includes ensuring that the media has access to pertinent information and key individuals for interviews, which in turn can affect the coverage of the event and the perception of the sports program. Effective media relations require a keen understanding of the media landscape and the ability to anticipate and manage the public's expectations. By maintaining a positive public image and skillfully shaping the narratives that emerge around their athletic programs and athletes, sports departments can influence public opinion, bolster community support, and elevate the profile of the institution as a whole. These efforts can create a mutually beneficial relationship between the media and collegiate sports programs, one where the flow of information supports the advancement of the institution's goals and honors the dedication of its athletes.

Digital Media and Fan Engagement

The surge of digital media has revolutionized sport communication, especially in the collegiate arena where the connection with the fan base is integral to the program's vibrancy. Athletic departments have embraced platforms such as Twitter, Instagram, and Facebook, not just as broadcasting channels, but as community spaces where fans can interact, share experiences, and feel more connected to their favorite teams and athletes. This digital engagement transcends geographical barriers, enabling fans to participate in game-day experiences and behind-the-scenes action regardless of physical proximity. As a result, social media has become an essential tool in not only maintaining but also expanding the fan base by delivering personalized content that resonates with the diverse interests of supporters, fostering a year-round engagement with the athletic brand.

In addition to enhancing fan experience, digital media is pivotal for brand building in collegiate athletics. Athletic departments craft strategic content that highlights the ethos and achievements of their sports programs, aligning with institutional values and broadening their reach to potential recruits and stakeholders. Through curated stories, highlight reels, and interactive campaigns, these digital platforms provide a narrative that goes beyond wins and losses, encapsulating the holistic journey of student-athletes and the spirit of the institution. This engagement is crucial not only during the active seasons but also in the off-season, where the focus shifts to training, academic accomplishments, and community involvement, keeping the momentum alive and fans invested throughout the year.

Crisis Communication

Crisis communication within collegiate athletics demands both a proactive strategy and a reactive agility. Athletic departments must anticipate potential crises and develop comprehensive communication plans that address a range of scenarios, from individual player issues to widespread institutional challenges. The cornerstone of effective crisis management is a prepared communication department that can swiftly enact its crisis plan, maintaining control over the narrative and disseminating clear, accurate information to the public. This involves not just drafting potential press releases in advance but also role-playing responses to various scenarios to ensure that when a crisis does strike, the response is measured, timely, and in alignment with the institution's values. It's crucial that these plans are revisited regularly and adapted to reflect the evolving social and media landscapes, as well as the unique dynamics of the institution and its athletic programs.

In moments of crisis, the immediate response can shape the public's long-term perception of the institution. A well-crafted communication plan involves identifying the spokesperson, crafting messages that resonate with key stakeholders, and establishing channels for timely dissemination of information. Training for staff extends beyond the communication department, ensuring that all potential points of contact within the athletic department are equipped to handle inquiries with a unified voice. Regular training keeps these skills sharp and helps to mitigate the risks of miscommunication or escalation of the crisis. Furthermore, in today's digital age, monitoring online sentiment and responding to concerns through social media is an integral part of crisis communication, allowing for rapid response and engagement with the community to reassure, clarify, and retain public trust.

Compliance and Communication

In collegiate athletics, the intertwining of compliance and communication underscores the importance of adhering to NCAA regulations while effectively conveying the institution's values and objectives. Compliance officers, in collaboration with communication professionals, are tasked with the critical responsibility of ensuring that all forms of communication, whether it's recruitment announcements, press releases, or social media updates, are in strict adherence to NCAA rules. This is particularly crucial in areas such as recruitment, where specific guidelines dictate the manner and timing of communication with prospective student-athletes. Moreover, the protection of student-athlete privacy remains a top priority, necessitating a nuanced approach to information sharing that respects both regulatory requirements and the individual's right to privacy.

The introduction of Name, Image, and Likeness (NIL) legislation presents new challenges and opportunities within the domain of collegiate sports communication. Compliance and communication teams must navigate these complexities by staying informed about evolving NIL policies and crafting messages that support student-athletes in their personal brand endeavors, all while maintaining the educational integrity of the athletic program. The careful balance between empowering athletes to leverage their NIL and ensuring institutional compliance requires transparent and ongoing dialogue between compliance officers, communication teams, and the athletes themselves. Through this collaborative approach, institutions can foster an environment where compliance is seamlessly integrated into the narrative of the sports program, reinforcing the institution's commitment to excellence both on and off the field.

Internal Communication and Organizational Culture

In the realm of collegiate athletics, internal communication is the sinew that connects and supports the various segments of an organization, fostering a culture of unity and shared purpose. It's through deliberate and consistent internal messaging that departments such as coaching, marketing, and compliance can synchronize their efforts towards common institutional goals. By promoting open dialogue and transparency within the organization, internal communication ensures that all stakeholders are informed and aligned with the athletic department's objectives, strategic decisions, and policy changes. This alignment is essential, as it not only enhances the efficiency of operations but also helps to forge a cohesive organizational culture that can significantly contribute to the success of athletic programs.

Organizational culture in collegiate athletics is built on the foundation of shared beliefs, values, and practices that characterize how an institution's sports entities operate. Effective internal communication upholds and disseminates these cultural elements, reinforcing the identity and ethos of the department. This includes celebrating achievements, recognizing individual and team contributions, and addressing challenges collaboratively. By fostering a positive, inclusive, and high-performing culture through strategic communication, athletic departments can motivate staff, instill pride, and encourage a collective responsibility towards the athletic program's reputation and success. Internal communication thus becomes an essential tool in cultivating a culture that not only values winning on the field but also emphasizes integrity, academic excellence, and the overall development of student-athletes.

The Future of Sports Communication and the NCAA

The realm of NCAA sports communication is on the cusp of significant evolution, driven by technological advancements and changing consumer media habits. In the near future, we can expect the integration of augmented and virtual reality technologies to not only enhance fan experience but also open new channels for storytelling and fan engagement. As the generation of digital natives moves into college and becomes the core audience for NCAA programs, there will be an increasing demand for more interactive, on-demand, and personalized content. This shift is likely to compel sports communication professionals to adapt to new tools and platforms, leveraging virtual environments for training, recruiting, and fan interactions. The rise of esports and its integration into collegiate athletics also signals an expansion of the traditional definition of sports, requiring communicators to broaden their skills and strategies to encompass these new domains.

The proliferation of digital platforms will necessitate a greater emphasis on content strategies that resonate across diverse mediums, from social media to mobile apps and beyond. As analytics become more refined, the NCAA's communication strategies will likely become more data-driven, utilizing fan insights to tailor content and engagement strategies effectively. This will enable institutions to deliver high-value experiences that keep fans connected year-round, not just during the sports seasons. Privacy and personalization will become key considerations, with the challenge being to balance the use of data to enhance fan experiences without infringing on personal privacy. Additionally, as issues like athlete compensation and the mental health of student-athletes gain prominence, transparent and responsible communication will become even more critical.

Finally, as NCAA sports communication evolves, the role of compliance will also transform. The NCAA will need to navigate the complex waters of digital rights, intellectual property, and the monetization of athlete likenesses, especially in the wake of new Name, Image, and Likeness (NIL) legislation. Communication teams will need to work in closer alignment with legal and compliance departments to ensure that all public messaging, digital campaigns, and athlete promotions adhere to evolving regulations. This will also mean providing robust education to student-athletes, who are now content creators and brand ambassadors in their own right, equipping them with the knowledge and tools to navigate their personal brands within the NCAA framework. The future of NCAA sports communication is not just about adapting to new technologies but also about fostering an environment where innovation, education, and compliance go hand-in-hand.

Discussion Questions

- How can collegiate athletic departments balance the need for publicity with the responsibility of upholding the privacy and well-being of student-athletes?
- In what ways can digital media be leveraged to enhance fan engagement and support for lesser-known sports within a collegiate athletic program?
- What are the best practices for sport communication professionals when responding to a crisis within a collegiate athletic department?
- How can NCAA communication strategies be redesigned to take advantage of virtual and augmented reality technologies while still aligning with the organization's core values?
- What are the ethical implications of using advanced data analytics and AI in sports communication, and how can NCAA ensure the privacy and rights of student-athletes are protected?
- How can the NCAA balance traditional and emerging communication platforms to cater to a diverse audience, including digital natives and traditional sports fans?
- As the landscape of collegiate athletics evolves, how should the NCAA adapt its crisis communication plans to address potential issues related to new technologies and digital media?
- What role should student-athletes play in shaping the communication strategies of their institutions, particularly with regard to their own personal brands and the use of their Name, Image, and Likeness (NIL)?
- How can collegiate athletic programs use social media responsibly and effectively to highlight the academic achievements and community involvement of student-athletes alongside their athletic performance?

- In the wake of NIL legislation, how can the NCAA ensure that communication strategies around athlete endorsements and partnerships remain compliant with the new rules and regulations?

Case Study 16.1: Crisis Communication in Response to a Data Breach

Big State University (BSU) prides itself on its successful collegiate athletic programs, which are a source of school spirit and community engagement. The university has invested heavily in digital platforms to promote its teams and to engage with fans, students, and alumni. They maintain a robust database that includes sensitive information on student-athletes, including academic records, health information, and personal identifiers.

The Event
In March, a sophisticated cyber-attack targeted BSU's athletic department, resulting in a data breach. Hackers gained access to the department's database, potentially compromising the personal data of hundreds of student-athletes. Upon discovery, the BSU communication team quickly engaged its crisis communication plan, which included a coordinated response with the university's IT department, notifications to affected individuals, and a public statement outlining the nature of the breach and steps taken to address it.

The Impact
The data breach and subsequent response received significant media attention, affecting the public's trust in BSU's ability to protect student information. There was a notable impact on the recruitment process as prospective athletes and their parents expressed concern over privacy issues. Additionally, there was a temporary decline in fan engagement on digital platforms, indicating a loss of confidence from the community.

Discussion
- How could BSU have better prepared for a potential data breach, and what preventive measures should be implemented in the future?
- In what ways can BSU's athletic department restore trust with its student-athletes, fans, and prospective recruits after the breach?
- What are the long-term implications for BSU's brand and its digital engagement initiatives following the data breach?
- How can BSU ensure compliance with NCAA regulations and privacy laws when communicating about the breach to the public?
- What role can student-athletes play in shaping the narrative around the university's response to the crisis?

Case Study 16.2: Leveraging Media for Underrepresented Sports

The University of Innovation (UI) is known for its dominant football and basketball programs. However, its lesser-known sports like lacrosse, volleyball, and track have struggled to gain attention and support. Recognizing the potential of digital media, UI's athletic department decided to revamp its approach to fan engagement, aiming to elevate the profile of these sports within the collegiate landscape.

The Event
UI launched a digital media campaign called "Spotlight Sports" with a dedicated team to create engaging content for underrepresented sports. This included behind-the-scenes footage, athlete profiles, live-tweeting during events, and interactive online competitions to win tickets and merchandise. The campaign used analytics to tailor content to user preferences and employed hashtags to track engagement.

The Impact
The "Spotlight Sports" campaign led to a significant increase in online engagement, with a notable rise in attendance at events for the featured sports. Athletes from these sports reported an increase in personal motivation and appreciation due to the recognition they were receiving. The campaign also attracted local sponsors interested in targeting the engaged demographic, providing an additional revenue stream for the athletic department.

Discussion
- How can UI measure the long-term success of the "Spotlight Sports" campaign beyond initial fan engagement metrics?
- What strategies can UI employ to ensure the sustainability of this increased attention to underrepresented sports?
- In what ways can the athletes from these lesser-known sports be involved in content creation to further personalize fan engagement?
- How can UI's athletic department balance the promotion of underrepresented sports without detracting from the visibility of its flagship football and basketball programs?
- What lessons can other universities learn from UI's approach to promoting underrepresented sports through digital media?

Chapter 17
NIL, Transfer Portal, Super Conferences, and the Future of the NCAA

The landscape of college sports is undergoing a seismic shift, driven by changes in student-athlete compensation, transfer regulations, conference realignment, and the existential challenges facing the NCAA. This chapter explores these developments, offering insights into their implications for the future of intercollegiate athletics.

Upon successful completion of this unit, students will be able to:

- Understand the implications of NIL policies on athlete compensation, recruitment strategies, and the collegiate sports landscape.
- Analyze the effects of the transfer portal on team dynamics, athlete mobility, and competitive balance within college athletics.
- Explore the emergence of super conferences and their impact on traditional rivalries, financial disparities, and NCAA governance.
- Examine the challenges and opportunities presented by the changing regulatory environment for NIL, including ethical considerations and the need for uniform policies.
- Investigate the potential for NCAA reforms in response to the evolving dynamics of athlete compensation, transfer rules, and conference realignment.
- Assess the future of the NCAA and intercollegiate athletics in light of recent developments in athlete rights, conference power structures, and the broader sports economy.

Name, Image, and Likeness (NIL)

The NIL era marks a departure from the strict amateurism model that has long governed college sports. Enabled by landmark legal decisions and state legislation, student-athletes can now profit from their personal brand without jeopardizing their eligibility. This evolution challenges the NCAA's traditional revenue model and introduces new dynamics in athlete recruitment and university sports programs.

Impact on Recruitment and Competitive Balance

In the new era of collegiate sports, Name, Image, and Likeness (NIL) has become a game-changing factor in the recruitment of student-athletes. The ability for athletes to monetize their personal brand has established a new front in the competition among universities to attract top talent. Historically dominant programs with vast alumni networks and marketing prowess can now leverage these assets to provide more lucrative NIL opportunities. This financial incentivization adds another layer to the recruitment process, often tipping the scales in favor of schools with the means to facilitate high-value endorsements and partnerships. The emergence of NIL collectives, serving as intermediaries between athletes and commercial interests, intensifies this disparity. These organizations, often backed by affluent boosters, create a competitive edge by ensuring lucrative deals that further attract elite recruits to already resource-rich programs.

The impact of NIL on the competitive balance in college sports is profound and multifaceted. While it offers student-athletes unprecedented opportunities to benefit from their skills and marketability, it also risks widening the gap between programs. Smaller schools, which may not have the financial muscle or the commercial appeal of their bigger counterparts, find themselves at a disadvantage, struggling to compete on this new financial playing field. This could lead to a concentration of talent at wealthier institutions, potentially stifling diversity and competition within college sports. Moreover, the increased focus on personal gain may overshadow the traditional values of college athletics, such as team cohesion, educational priorities, and the amateur spirit of competition. As the NIL landscape continues to evolve, the challenge will be to maintain an equitable environment where all programs can compete, and student-athletes can make decisions that benefit their future, both on and off the field.

Ethical and Regulatory Challenges

The implementation of NIL policies presents a complex ethical landscape in collegiate athletics, marked by a multitude of stakeholder interests and the significant potential for conflicts of interest and exploitation. With student-athletes now able to engage in commercial ventures, the lines between amateurism and professionalism blur, raising questions about the integrity of the educational mission of colleges and universities. Ethical challenges arise when athletes, potentially unsophisticated in business matters, navigate endorsement deals, potentially without adequate guidance. Moreover, the presence of deep-pocketed donors and businesses around collegiate programs creates an environment ripe for undue influence, where the line between legitimate NIL activities and improper inducements or pay-for-play scenarios is perilously thin. Without clear regulations and robust oversight, these challenges threaten the fairness and level playing field that are foundational to sports.

Compounding these ethical concerns is a fragmented regulatory environment, with the NCAA, individual conferences, and various state legislatures each promulgating their own NIL guidelines. This lack of uniformity can lead to confusion and inconsistency, hindering the effective governance of NIL activities. There is a pressing need for a comprehensive policy framework that can provide clarity, prevent abuses, and protect the welfare of student-athletes. Such a framework must balance the need for athlete autonomy and the opportunity to benefit from their own name, image, and likeness, with the risk of corrupt practices that could undermine the integrity of collegiate sports. It is imperative that any regulatory approach be guided by the principles of fairness, transparency, and equity, ensuring that all student-athletes, irrespective of sport or division level, can navigate the NIL landscape with confidence and security.

NCAA Transfer Portal

The NCAA's relaxation of transfer rules has led to an unprecedented mobility among student-athletes. The transfer portal, allowing athletes to change schools without sitting out a season, has democratized athlete movement but also introduced challenges.

Effects on Team Dynamics and Loyalty

The NCAA Transfer Portal has dramatically altered the collegiate athletic landscape, introducing an era where student-athletes have the flexibility to transfer schools without the traditional restrictions. While this system empowers athletes with agency over their athletic careers, it introduces significant challenges for team dynamics and loyalty. The ease of transferring can disrupt the fabric of a team, as athletes may now readily depart in pursuit of more playing time, better financial aid packages, or a more prominent program. This shift towards a free-market approach can lead to a transactional mindset, weakening the sense of commitment that is often central to team cohesion and success. Coaches and athletic programs must now operate in a fluid environment where roster stability is no longer a given, and the traditional cultivation of athlete loyalty over years may be diminished by immediate opportunities elsewhere.

From a coaching perspective, the Transfer Portal demands a recalibration of strategies for team building and program development. Coaches are tasked with fostering a competitive environment that encourages athletes to stay, while also navigating the potential influx of transfer talent that could fill immediate needs. This requires a delicate balance between developing homegrown talent and integrating transfers who may only be part of the program for a limited time. The transient nature of rosters can pose a challenge to the long-term vision of a program, as the constant turnover requires coaches to adapt quickly and blend new personalities and skill sets. The priority becomes maintaining a competitive team culture that both nurtures loyalty and accommodates the dynamic nature of modern college athletics.

Opportunities and Risks for Athletes

The NCAA Transfer Portal, while designed to give student-athletes more autonomy and control over their collegiate careers, presents a complex array of opportunities and risks. For athletes, the portal can be a gateway to new beginnings, offering the chance to find a better fit academically, athletically, or culturally. This empowerment aligns with the modern view of student-athletes as individuals with the right to shape their own destinies. However, the allure of potential opportunities can sometimes be misleading. Not every transfer leads to increased playing time, a better team situation, or enhanced exposure to professional scouts. Moreover, the impact on academic progression can be significant, as transferring can disrupt degree completion timelines and scholarship eligibility, potentially leaving athletes in precarious positions both on the field and in the classroom.

Navigating the Transfer Portal requires careful consideration and robust support systems to mitigate risks. Athletes must evaluate a multitude of factors, including compatibility with new coaches, team dynamics, and the academic offerings of potential schools. Without proper guidance, there is a danger of making ill-informed decisions based on short-term gains rather than long-term career and educational outcomes.

Consequently, the role of academic advisors, compliance officers, and coaches becomes critical in providing comprehensive support, ensuring that student-athletes are fully aware of the implications of transferring. Such support is not only essential in assisting athletes through the transfer process but also in helping them understand the long-term consequences of their decisions on their personal development and post-collegiate aspirations.

Super Conferences and Realignment

The consolidation of power among a few "super conferences" is reshaping the collegiate sports landscape. Driven by television revenues and market expansion, conference realignment threatens traditional rivalries and regional affiliations, raising questions about the future role and relevance of the NCAA.

Financial Implications and Accessibility

The advent of NCAA super conferences has ushered in an era where the financial muscle of a select few collegiate athletic programs dictates the success and viability of teams within the broader NCAA framework. These super conferences, with their lucrative media deals and expansive marketing platforms, funnel unprecedented levels of wealth and exposure to their member institutions. The financial boon enjoyed by these elite conferences translates into state-of-the-art facilities, top-tier coaching staff, and a recruiting allure that smaller programs simply cannot match. The disparity is not merely financial but also extends to the accessibility of top talent, as recruits gravitate towards the visibility and potential for career advancement offered by super conference teams. The chasm created by this concentration of resources threatens to leave less affluent programs, which are unable to compete financially, on the peripheries of college sports, struggling to remain relevant and competitive.

This concentration of resources and opportunities creates a two-tier system within the NCAA, where accessibility to the upper echelons of collegiate sports becomes increasingly difficult for programs outside the super conference constellation. Smaller schools face the daunting task of maintaining competitive athletic programs with far fewer resources, often relying on creativity and a more communal approach to funding. As super conferences continue to capitalize on their economic advantages, the challenge for the NCAA is to ensure that all member institutions retain the opportunity to compete on a somewhat level playing field. This requires innovative approaches to revenue sharing, scholarship allocations, and facilities upgrades, allowing lesser-funded programs the chance to remain viable contenders. In the absence of such interventions, the essence of college sports—its spirit of competition and opportunity—may become eclipsed by the wide financial gaps among its participants.

Governance and Autonomy

The landscape of NCAA governance is experiencing tectonic shifts as the emergence of super conferences cultivates a new paradigm of autonomy and control. The consolidation of power within these conferences has begun to challenge the historical centrality of the NCAA, presenting a possible future where governance is highly decentralized. With super conferences increasingly dictating their own rules and negotiating their own lucrative media contracts, the role of the NCAA as the central regulatory body comes into question. This trend extends beyond financial aspects, permeating into areas such as athlete compensation, health and safety protocols, and academic standards. Such autonomy could lead to disparate sets of rules and regulations across the collegiate landscape, potentially complicating national competition and undermining the uniformity that the NCAA has traditionally sought to uphold.

As super conferences continue to fortify their positions, a debate over the need for a new regulatory framework ensues, one that can reconcile the desire for autonomy with the need for a coherent national structure for college sports. The NCAA finds itself at a crossroads, tasked with redefining its authority and the extent of its oversight in a way that harmonizes with the newfound independence of super conferences. This may involve a restructuring of its governance model to allow for more input and flexibility for conferences while maintaining a level of oversight to ensure fair competition and the well-being of student-athletes. It necessitates a delicate balance between allowing conferences the freedom to innovate and preserving the interconnectivity and shared standards that support the broader goals of college athletics. In navigating this complex terrain, the NCAA must engage with a wide array of stakeholders to develop a governance structure that is both adaptive to the evolving nature of college sports and respectful of the diverse interests of its members.

The Future of the NCAA and Intercollegiate Athletics

As intercollegiate athletics confront the profound changes brought about by NIL policies, the transfer portal, and the creation of super conferences, the NCAA stands at a pivotal juncture. The organization must embark on a journey of self-reflection and reinvention to continue to play a meaningful role in the future of college sports. This reinvention will necessitate the NCAA to fundamentally reassess and adapt its governance structures, aiming for a more transparent, responsive, and athlete-centered approach. The NCAA must serve not only as a regulatory body but also as an advocate for the welfare of student-athletes, balancing the commercial aspects of modern sports with the educational and developmental missions of its member institutions.

Comprehensive reforms addressing athlete compensation, the facilitation and regulation of transfers, and the preservation of competitive balance are critical in this new era. The NCAA must navigate these challenges with a collaborative spirit, engaging with athletes, coaches, administrators, and lawmakers to forge equitable standards that uphold the integrity of sports while protecting the interests and rights of all athletes. These reforms should aim to provide clarity and fairness to the rules surrounding athlete compensation and movement, ensuring that the landscape of college sports remains both competitive and just. This may include establishing a universal code for NIL activities, creating clear pathways for transfers that consider the athletes' academic progress, and ensuring that the drive for revenue does not overshadow the spirit of competition.

The future of college sports depends significantly on the NCAA's capacity to innovate and inclusively represent its diverse membership. An inclusive approach that respects the varying needs and strengths of different programs and athletes will be crucial. The organization must champion the core educational values that underpin the collegiate model, ensuring that the holistic development of student-athletes remains at the forefront. By doing so, the NCAA can reinforce the importance of intercollegiate athletics as a complement to the academic experience, fostering environments where sports serve as a conduit for personal growth, leadership, and community building.

In sustaining the integrity and appeal of college sports, the NCAA must acknowledge and integrate the realities of a rapidly evolving sports industry. Embracing technological advancements, new media landscapes, and changing societal expectations about athlete rights will be vital in this endeavor. The NCAA's willingness to adapt its practices and policies to reflect these changes will be indicative of its commitment to remaining a central figure in the athletic, academic, and personal lives of student-athletes. This will require a forward-looking vision that aligns with the long-term interests of sports as a whole, including the fans, institutions, and the communities they inspire.

The transformation of college sports presents a spectrum of challenges and opportunities. By embracing change and prioritizing equity, the NCAA and its member institutions can chart a course toward a vibrant and sustainable future for intercollegiate athletics. This future hinges on a collective commitment to adapt, engage in meaningful dialogue, and enact changes that resonate with the values and aspirations of the athletic community. With concerted effort and visionary leadership, the NCAA can foster an environment that continues to celebrate the tradition of college sports while embracing the modern era with open arms.

Discussion Questions

- How do NIL policies impact the traditional concept of amateurism in NCAA athletics, and what should the NCAA's role be in regulating these policies?
- In what ways can the NCAA ensure that NIL opportunities do not compromise the academic integrity and educational priorities of student-athletes?
- Considering the ease of transferring facilitated by the NCAA Transfer Portal, how might this affect an athlete's commitment to a team and their educational journey?
- How should NCAA governance adapt to accommodate the increasing autonomy and influence of super conferences while ensuring competitive balance?
- With the current trajectory of decentralization, what steps can the NCAA take to maintain a semblance of control and oversight over collegiate athletics?
- In a landscape where financial disparities are growing due to super conferences, what measures can be taken to protect smaller programs and promote equity?
- What are the potential consequences of the transfer portal on team culture and long-term program development, and how might coaches and administrators mitigate these effects?
- How could the NCAA foster collaborative efforts among various stakeholders to establish equitable standards for athlete compensation and transfers?
- As super conferences continue to evolve, what could be the potential challenges and benefits of these entities gaining more autonomy over college sports?
- What role should the NCAA play in ensuring that the holistic development of student-athletes remains a priority amid the changing dynamics of intercollegiate athletics?
- What are the implications of NIL and transfer portal policies on the recruitment process and the overall student-athlete experience?
- How can the NCAA create a regulatory environment that accommodates the interests of its diverse membership while maintaining a level playing field?
- Discuss the potential impact of athlete mobility on the traditional rivalries and regional affiliations in NCAA sports. How important are

these aspects to the identity and appeal of college sports?

- Reflect on the future trajectory of the NCAA and propose strategies that could help sustain its relevance and effectiveness in overseeing intercollegiate athletics.

Case Study 17.1: The Rise of NIL and Its Impact on a Mid-Major Program

The advent of Name, Image, and Likeness (NIL) legislation represents a tectonic shift in the NCAA's amateurism model, allowing student-athletes to profit from their personal brand. This has disrupted traditional recruitment methods and posed new challenges for NCAA governance. Mid-major athletic programs, often with fewer resources than their Power 5 counterparts, must navigate this changing landscape.

The Event

In the fall of 2023, Riverside University, a mid-major school with a strong basketball history, faced the reality of NIL. The university's star player, Jason Carter, was approached with an NIL deal worth $100,000 from a local car dealership. The deal required significant social media promotion and personal appearances, raising concerns about Carter's time management and potential NCAA violations due to the ambiguous state laws on NIL.

The Impact

Carter's NIL deal sparked immediate changes at Riverside. Other athletes began seeking similar deals, creating tensions among teams. The university faced the complex task of establishing compliance protocols for NIL activities without state guidelines. Local businesses, eager to tap into the school's athletic fame, inundated athletes with endorsement proposals. Riverside's athletic department had to quickly adapt to provide oversight and education for its student-athletes to navigate these deals.

Discussion

- How can mid-major programs like Riverside University support their athletes in pursuing NIL deals while ensuring compliance with NCAA rules?
- What steps should Riverside take to educate both local businesses and student-athletes about the ethical considerations of NIL arrangements?
- How might Jason Carter's high-profile NIL deal affect team dynamics, and what can coaches do to maintain team cohesion?
- In what ways does the introduction of NIL require a reevaluation of the traditional student-athlete model, particularly at mid-major institutions?

- Should the NCAA consider implementing a uniform NIL policy to minimize disparities among different state laws, and if so, what should be the key elements of such a policy?

Case Study 17.2: Transfer Portal Turmoil and Team Turnaround

The Transfer Portal has become a significant feature of the NCAA landscape, providing student-athletes the freedom to transfer schools with fewre strictions. This has led to increased athlete mobility but also introduced complexities related to team dynamics and program loyalty.

The Event
Hawthorne College, a Division I school known for its competitive soccer program, found itself in turmoil when six key players entered the Transfer Portal at the end of the 2023 season. The departures were spurred by the promise of better exposure, facilities, and playing opportunities at larger programs. This exodus forced the head coach, Alex Martinez, to reconsider recruitment strategies and address the remaining team's morale.

The Impact
The mass departure left Hawthorne with gaps in key positions and a dwindling roster as the new season approached. To rebuild, Coach Martinez focused on recruiting overlooked talent, emphasizing the potential for immediate playtime and personal development. Simultaneously, the athletic department developed enhanced support structures for athlete development, including mentorship programs and leadership training. By the season's midpoint, the restructured team had surpassed expectations, demonstrating improved cohesion and resilience, ultimately achieving a winning record that became a rallying point for the entire school community.

Discussion
- How can smaller programs like Hawthorne College mitigate the impact of the Transfer Portal on their team rosters and maintain a competitive program?
- What support systems can be implemented to address the concerns of student-athletes that might lead them to consider transferring?
- How might Hawthorne's approach to recruiting and team culture change as a result of their experience with the Transfer Portal?
- What are the ethical responsibilities of larger programs in recruiting athletes from smaller schools through the Transfer Portal?
- In what ways could the NCAA regulate the Transfer Portal to ensure fair competition and protect the interests of both student-athletes and athletic programs?

Chapter 18
Youth, Community, and High School Athletics

Community and high school athletics embody a vital aspect of youth development, offering avenues for physical, social, and emotional growth. This chapter explores the organizational frameworks, participation dynamics, and the overarching governance that shapes high school and community sports landscapes.

Upon successful completion of this unit, students will be able to:

- Identify the key organizational structures and administrative challenges of community and high school sports programs, including funding, resource allocation, and volunteer engagement.
- Analyze the role and impact of state high school athletic associations and the National Federation of State High School Associations (NFHS) in governing high school sports, including their influence on rules, regulations, and eligibility criteria.
- Discuss the significance of high school athletics in the broader context of student development, including its effects on academic performance, social skills, and personal growth.
- Evaluate the strategies employed by community and high school sports programs to overcome operational challenges, including facility maintenance, equipment provision, and logistical considerations.
- Recognize the importance of community support, fundraising, and sponsorships in sustaining and enhancing community and high school sports programs.
- Assess the ethical considerations and decision-making processes involved in the administration of high school sports, particularly regarding gender equity, inclusivity, and the balance between competitive success and participant enjoyment.

Community Sports Organization

Community sports leagues serve as a vital component of local communities, offering structured environments where individuals, particularly youth, can engage in physical activities, learn teamwork, and develop social connections. By offering a range of sports, these leagues cater to diverse interests and skill levels, making sports accessible to all segments of the community. The choice between single-sport focus and multi-sport offerings allows organizations to tailor their programs to meet the specific needs and preferences of their community members. This flexibility not only enhances participation rates but also encourages a lifelong engagement with physical activity, promoting healthier lifestyles among participants.

However, the operation of community sports leagues is not without its challenges. Securing adequate funding is a perennial concern, as these leagues often rely on a mix of participant fees, community donations, and sponsorship deals to cover operational costs. These financial resources are essential for maintaining facilities, purchasing equipment, and ensuring that participation fees remain affordable to encourage broad community involvement. In addition to financial hurdles, effective resource management is critical, requiring careful planning and organization to optimize the use of available facilities, schedule events and matches, and manage the logistics of league operation.

Volunteer mobilization is another crucial aspect of running a successful community sports league. Volunteers often serve in various capacities, including coaching, officiating, event organization, and administrative support. Recruiting and retaining a dedicated volunteer base can be challenging, necessitating a focus on volunteer recognition, support, and development to build a strong community spirit. The ability of a league to mobilize and sustain a committed group of volunteers directly impacts its capacity to offer enriching sports programs and contributes to the overall health and vibrancy of the community.

High School Sports

High school athletics play a pivotal role in the educational journey of many students, offering a platform where the values of hard work, dedication, and collaboration are not just encouraged but exemplified. Beyond the physical benefits, high school sports are instrumental in teaching students life skills that are critical for success beyond the classroom and the field. In an environment where the pressure to perform academically can be overwhelming, athletics provide a much-needed outlet for stress, a sense of belonging, and an opportunity for personal achievement. The upward trend in participation reflects a growing acknowledgment among educators, parents, and students themselves of the myriad benefits that sports offer, including improved academic performance, higher self-esteem, and better overall mental health.

The lessons learned through high school sports—teamwork, discipline, and perseverance—are invaluable and often life-altering. Team sports, in particular, teach students how to work towards a common goal with individuals from diverse backgrounds and with varying levels of skill. Discipline learned on the field translates into self-discipline in academic pursuits and personal life, teaching students the importance of time management, commitment, and hard work. Perseverance through challenging practices and losses builds resilience, preparing students to face life's obstacles with determination and grit. Thus, high school athletics not only complement academic learning but are fundamental in shaping well-rounded, capable individuals ready to contribute positively to society.

Governance in High School Athletics

The National Federation of State High School Associations (NFHS) serves as the cornerstone for high school athletics and activities across the United States. As a national authority, the NFHS develops rules of play for sports, provides guidance on administrative and operational issues, and establishes standards for the conduct of participants and spectators alike. Its mission is not only to ensure that high school sports are competitive and fair but also to foster an environment where the educational values of sports are recognized and upheld. By offering a comprehensive framework of rules and guidelines, the NFHS ensures that high school athletics remain an integral part of the educational experience, emphasizing the development of leadership, health, and citizenship among student-athletes.

The NFHS works closely with state high school athletic associations, such as the Utah High School Activities Association (UHSAA), to implement and adapt its guidelines to meet the unique needs of each state's schools and student populations. This partnership is essential for maintaining a standardized approach to high school athletics while allowing for necessary flexibility at the state level. State associations like the UHSAA are responsible for the day-to-day administration of high school sports within their jurisdictions, including the scheduling of competitions, the training and certification of officials, and the enforcement of eligibility criteria and sportsmanship standards. The support and standards provided by the NFHS enable state associations to execute their responsibilities effectively and ensure a consistent and equitable sporting experience for all participants.

One of the key areas where the NFHS and state associations collaborate is in the development and updating of sports rules. The NFHS regularly reviews and revises its rulebooks for each sport, considering changes in the sports themselves as well as advances in safety and protective equipment. State associations, drawing on their direct experience with schools, coaches, and athletes, provide valuable feedback and suggestions to the NFHS during this process. This cooperative approach ensures that the rules of play remain relevant, safe, and conducive to fair competition. For example, the UHSAA might work with the NFHS to adapt basketball rules that address specific concerns related to player safety that have arisen within Utah, ensuring that student-athletes are protected while maintaining the integrity of the game.

Eligibility criteria are another critical area of governance where the NFHS and state associations work hand in hand. The NFHS establishes broad eligibility guidelines based on age, enrollment status, academic achievement, and residence, among other factors. State associations, like the UHSAA, then tailor these guidelines to fit the context of their schools and communities. This system ensures that students across the country meet a baseline level of eligibility while allowing state associations the latitude to address local issues and concerns. For instance, the UHSAA might implement additional academic requirements or transfer rules that reflect the values and expectations of Utah's educational community.

Finally, the NFHS plays a crucial role in promoting sportsmanship, education-based athletics, and the overall development of student-athletes. Through national conferences, educational materials, and leadership programs, the NFHS provides state associations with the tools they need to foster positive sports environments. State associations, in turn, implement these programs at the local level, customizing them to resonate with their schools and communities. The UHSAA, for example, might adopt NFHS sportsmanship initiatives, integrating them into training programs for coaches and athletes, to ensure that the principles of respect, integrity, and responsibility are upheld in all aspects of high school athletics in Utah.

Through this collaborative and multi-layered approach to governance, the NFHS and state associations like the UHSAA ensure that high school sports in the United States are not only competitive and enjoyable but also deeply educational experiences that contribute to the growth and development of young people.

Working with Prep Schools

Preparatory academies and charter schools are specialized educational institutions designed to provide alternative learning environments and curriculums compared to traditional public schools. Prep academies often focus on rigorous academic preparation, aiming to equip students for higher education with a strong emphasis on college entrance exam performance and advanced subject matter expertise. Charter schools, while also offering unique educational approaches, operate with more autonomy from the standardized public school system, allowing for innovative teaching methods, specialized curriculums, and often a focus on specific themes or disciplines such as arts, technology, or science. Parents might choose to send their children to these institutions for a variety of reasons, including the desire for a more challenging academic environment, dissatisfaction with local public schools, the appeal of a particular educational philosophy, or the presence of specialized programs that better align with their child's interests and talents.

However, the distinct characteristics and operational frameworks of prep academies and charter schools often present challenges for student participation in high school sports. These schools may not be members of state high school athletic associations due to differing eligibility rules, academic schedules, or simply because their focus on specialized education does not prioritize athletics in the same way traditional public schools might. Additionally, the geographic location and smaller student body size of some prep academies and charter schools can make it logistically challenging to field competitive sports teams or join existing athletic conferences dominated by public schools. This exclusion from traditional high school sports participation means students at these institutions might miss out on the camaraderie, physical development, and leadership skills that come from being part of a team, driving some parents and schools to seek alternative athletic opportunities through club sports, independent leagues, or interscholastic competitions designed specifically for non-traditional schools.

State high school athletic associations often find themselves navigating the complex landscape of integrating preparatory schools and academies into the broader framework of high school athletics. These institutions typically operate with distinct academic calendars, curricular focuses, and athletic participation standards that differ significantly from those of public schools. Despite these differences, state associations are tasked with ensuring a level playing field where all institutions, regardless of their operational nuances, can compete fairly and equitably. This requires a delicate balance, as associations must adapt their regulations to accommodate the unique characteristics of preparatory schools and academies while maintaining the integrity and competitive balance of state-wide athletics. It involves continuous dialogue and cooperation between state associations and the administrations of these specialized institutions to align on eligibility rules, competition schedules, and transfer policies that respect the educational missions of all schools involved.

The relationship between state high school athletic associations and preparatory schools and academies underscores the associations' role in fostering inclusive, diverse, and equitable athletic environments. By working closely with these institutions, state associations can address and bridge the gaps in athletic participation standards, ensuring that student-athletes from various educational backgrounds have equal opportunities to compete and excel. This collaboration often leads to the development of tailored guidelines that recognize the unique academic commitments and athletic programming of preparatory schools and academies, thereby facilitating their integration into the state's athletic ecosystem. Moreover, this cooperation highlights the associations' commitment to supporting the holistic development of student-athletes, emphasizing the educational value of athletics across a broad spectrum of school settings and ensuring that the benefits of sports participation are accessible to a wide and diverse student population.

Administration of Community and High School Sports

The administration of community and high school sports programs requires a dynamic and comprehensive approach to ensure their success and sustainability. At the heart of these efforts is strategic planning, which encompasses everything from season scheduling, facility usage, and coordination with educational activities, to the long-term development of the sports programs themselves. Financial management plays a critical role, as administrators must budget for expenses such as uniforms, transportation, officiating fees, and facility upkeep, while also forecasting potential revenue streams from participation fees, gate receipts, and concession sales. Additionally, the logistical aspects of running sports programs, including team travel arrangements and event hosting, demand meticulous attention to detail and efficient resource allocation. The ultimate goal is to create an environment where student-athletes can thrive, developing their skills in a setting that supports their academic and athletic growth.

Community support is indispensable in the administration of these sports programs. Engaging local businesses, alumni, and families through effective communication and outreach efforts can bolster support for the programs, increasing attendance at events, and fostering a sense of pride and ownership within the community. Fundraising and sponsorships emerge as crucial elements in this landscape, providing necessary financial backing to supplement budgets and enable enhancements to the programs. Innovative fundraising campaigns, partnerships with local businesses, and alumni donations can all contribute to the financial health of sports programs. These efforts not only secure the resources needed for day-to-day operations but also facilitate improvements and expansions, such as upgrading facilities or adding new sports, which can have a profound impact on the quality of the athletic experience for students.

Moreover, the effective administration of community and high school sports programs requires a commitment to inclusivity and access. Ensuring that all students have the opportunity to participate, regardless of their financial situation, is a guiding principle for administrators. This may involve implementing sliding scale fees, offering scholarships, or organizing equipment drives to reduce the cost barriers to participation. By prioritizing accessibility and equity, administrators underscore the educational value of athletics, reinforcing the role of sports as a catalyst for personal development, teamwork, and community building. Ultimately, the successful administration of these programs hinges on a collaborative effort among administrators, coaches, parents, and the community at large, united by a shared vision of enriching the lives of young athletes through sports.

Discussion Questions

- How do the organizational structures of community sports leagues and high school sports programs differ, and what unique administrative challenges does each face?
- What is the role of the National Federation of State High School Associations (NFHS) in governing high school sports, and how does it collaborate with state associations like the Utah High School Activities Association (UHSAA) to standardize sports participation?
- Discuss the process by which the NFHS and state associations work together to develop and update sports rules. How does this collaboration ensure the safety and fairness of high school sports?
- How do state high school athletic associations tailor the NFHS's broad eligibility guidelines to fit their local contexts, and what are the implications of these adaptations for student-athletes?
- Examine the NFHS's role in promoting sportsmanship and education-based athletics. How do state associations implement these programs, and what impact do they have on the development of student-athletes?
- How do state high school athletic associations navigate the

integration of preparatory schools and academies, which have distinct academic calendars and athletic participation standards, into the broader framework of high school athletics?

- In the administration of community and high school sports, what strategies are employed to manage finances effectively, and how crucial are fundraising and sponsorships in maintaining and expanding these programs?
- Discuss the importance of community support in the administration of sports programs. How can effective communication and outreach bolster this support?
- How do administrators ensure inclusivity and access to sports programs for all students, regardless of their financial situation? What methods can be used to reduce cost barriers to participation?
- Considering the collaborative effort required among administrators, coaches, parents, and the community, what are some best practices for enriching the lives of young athletes through sports?

Case Study 18.1: Revitalizing a Community Through Youth Sports

In the small town of Greenfield, population 5,000, the local community sports league and high school athletics programs had seen better days. Limited funding, dwindling volunteer support, and outdated facilities had led to a decrease in participation rates among youth and high school students alike. Recognizing the vital role of sports in youth development and community engagement, a newly appointed director for the Greenfield Community Sports Program (GCSP) embarked on a mission to revitalize these athletic programs.

The Event
The GCSP director initiated a comprehensive strategic planning process, engaging stakeholders from across the community, including local businesses, schools, parents, and alumni. A significant breakthrough came when a local business coalition offered a substantial sponsorship deal, earmarked specifically for facility upgrades and equipment purchases. This funding, combined with a targeted volunteer recruitment drive and the implementation of sliding scale participation fees, led to a significant turnaround. New equipment was purchased, facilities were renovated, and for the first time in years, the league was able to offer scholarships to ensure that no child was left on the sidelines due to financial constraints. Additionally, the high school partnered with the GCSP to align their athletic schedules and share facilities, maximizing resources and fostering a stronger sports culture across all age groups.

The Impact

Within a year of these efforts, the GCSP saw a 40% increase in youth sports participation and a renewed sense of pride and enthusiasm for high school athletics among students. The upgraded facilities not only benefited the sports programs but also became a hub for community events, bringing residents together and fostering a sense of unity and pride in Greenfield. Furthermore, the emphasis on inclusivity and access led to a more diverse group of students participating in sports, contributing to an overall improvement in school and community spirit. The success of the GCSP also inspired other community initiatives, leading to a broader revitalization of Greenfield's public spaces and recreational programs.

Discussion

- How did strategic planning and community engagement contribute to the revitalization of the Greenfield Community Sports Program and high school athletics?
- In what ways can local businesses and community organizations collaborate to support youth and high school sports programs?
- What role do inclusivity and accessibility play in the success of community and high school sports programs, and how can these principles be effectively implemented?
- How can the success of the GCSP in revitalizing sports programs and community engagement serve as a model for other small towns facing similar challenges?
- Reflect on the long-term impact of improved sports facilities and programs on the overall development of youth and the quality of life in a community.

Case Study 18.2: Implementing a Holistic Student-Athlete Development Program in Rivertown High School

Rivertown High School, located in a medium-sized city with a diverse student population, faced challenges in balancing academic performance with athletic excellence. The school's sports teams were competitive, but there was growing concern among educators and parents that the focus on athletics was overshadowing academic achievement and personal development. In response, the school's athletic director, in collaboration with coaches, teachers, and a local university's sports psychology department, proposed a new initiative: the Holistic Student-Athlete Development Program (HSADP). The program aimed to integrate athletics, academics, and personal development activities to cultivate well-rounded student-athletes.

The Event

The HSADP was launched at the beginning of the academic year, featuring workshops on time management, study skills, mental health awareness, and leadership. Additionally, the program introduced a mentorship system, pairing younger athletes with senior students and alumni who had successfully balanced sports with academics and personal commitments. To support this initiative, the athletic department organized professional development sessions for coaches on fostering student-athlete growth beyond physical training. The program also included community service projects, encouraging teams to engage with local organizations and initiatives, thereby reinforcing the importance of civic responsibility and teamwork in real-world settings.

The Impact

By the end of the first year, Rivertown High School witnessed a noticeable improvement in student-athletes' academic performance, with grade point averages rising across all sports teams. Surveys among participants revealed increased levels of self-confidence, better stress management skills, and a stronger sense of belonging and purpose. Coaches reported more cohesive teams with athletes who were not only physically stronger but also more mentally resilient and engaged in their education and community. The success of the HSADP attracted attention from neighboring schools and districts, leading to discussions on implementing similar programs elsewhere. Moreover, the program strengthened the bond between the school and the wider community, highlighting the role of sports in developing civic-minded, academically successful, and mentally healthy young adults.

Discussion

- How did the Holistic Student-Athlete Development Program at Rivertown High School address the common challenge of balancing athletic and academic commitments among high school athletes?
- In what ways can mentorship from senior student-athletes and alumni contribute to the development of younger athletes, both in sports and in their personal lives?
- What role did professional development for coaches play in the success of the HSADP, and how can this be replicated in other high school athletic programs?
- How can integrating community service projects into high school sports programs benefit both the student-athletes and the local community?
- Reflect on the potential long-term impacts of programs like the HSADP on the culture of high school sports and the development of student-athletes.

Chapter 19
Common Roles in an NCAA Athletic Department

Modern NCAA athletic departments are complex entities requiring a diverse range of professionals to manage their multifaceted operations successfully. Common roles include the Athletic Director, who oversees the entire department; the Senior Woman Administrator, focusing on gender equity; and various assistant ADs responsible for compliance, facility management, and development. Other essential positions include the Business Manager, handling financial operations; the Marketing Director, driving fan engagement and branding initiatives; and the Director of Creative and New Media, leading digital content strategies. Together, these roles work synergistically to support student-athletes, enhance the department's brand, and ensure compliance with NCAA regulations, fostering a dynamic and successful athletic program.

Upon successful completion of this unit, students will be able to:

- Identify the key roles and responsibilities within a modern NCAA athletic department and understand their contribution to the department's overall success.
- Explain the importance of the Athletic Director's leadership in guiding the strategic direction and operational efficiency of the athletic department.
- Understand the functions of assistant athletic directors in areas such as compliance, facility management, and development, and how these areas contribute to the department's goals.
- Recognize the significance of financial management, marketing strategies, and creative media in enhancing the athletic department's brand, engaging fans, and ensuring financial sustainability.
- Analyze the collaborative nature of these roles and their interdependence in supporting student-athletes' academic and athletic success while maintaining compliance with NCAA regulations.

Athletic Director

Roles & Responsibilities

The Athletic Director (AD) plays a pivotal role in leading and administering the university's intercollegiate athletic program. Their primary goal is to support student-athletes and department employees in achieving their educational, professional, and personal life goals. This includes developing a synergistic partnership between the athletics department and various university units such as academic, student life, and administrative sections. Furthermore, the AD leads and administers the department's fundraising efforts in close collaboration with University Advancement, ensuring the financial health and sustainability of the athletic programs. The AD is also responsible for administering athletic and facilities budgets, making critical assessments and determinations regarding athletic programs, facility needs, equipment, and maintenance. An essential part of the role involves enhancing the positive public perception of the university and its athletic department, aligning the department's goals with the broader objectives of the institution, and fostering a culture of excellence and integrity within the sports programs.

Requirements

To qualify for the role of an Athletic Director, candidates must possess a minimum of a bachelor's degree, although a master's or doctoral degree are preferred. Additionally, progressive administrative experience in a university athletic program, business enterprise, or a closely related field is required. Strong interpersonal skills are crucial for this role, given the need for effective communication with various stakeholders including students, faculty, alumni, and the community. Experience in managing substantial budgets is necessary, along with fundraising and/or revenue generation, indicating the ability to secure financial resources for the department. The ability to create a collaborative work environment and develop strong partnerships within the university community and/or the community-at-large is essential for fostering a supportive ecosystem for athletic programs. College coaching and/or athletics administration experience is highly valued, along with a demonstrated commitment to gender equity and NCAA compliance, ensuring that the department operates within ethical and regulatory standards.

Business Management

Roles & Responsibilities

The Business Manager in an NCAA athletic department serves as the financial backbone of the organization, overseeing the financial operations and ensuring fiscal responsibility and compliance with both NCAA regulations and institutional policies. The business manager is responsible for preparing, managing, and monitoring the athletic department's budget, ensuring that all financial operations are transparent and in alignment with the department's goals and objectives. This includes forecasting revenue and expenses, managing cash flow, and performing regular financial analyses to guide strategic decision-making. They work closely with department heads and coaches to develop budgets for individual teams and ensure that spending aligns with allocated budgets. Additionally, the business manager oversees procurement processes, including negotiating contracts with vendors and suppliers for equipment, travel, and other services necessary for the department's operation. They are also responsible for payroll management for coaches and athletic department staff, ensuring timely and accurate compensation in compliance with university policies and employment laws. This role includes ensuring compliance with NCAA financial regulations, conducting internal audits, and preparing for external audits to ensure adherence to financial reporting requirements. They also play a key role in identifying and implementing cost-saving measures and revenue enhancement opportunities, working closely with development and fundraising staff to support financial goals.

Requirements

Candidates for this position typically require a bachelor's degree in business administration, finance, accounting, or a related field, with a preference for those holding a MBA or professional certifications such as CPA. Key skills include strong analytical and financial modeling abilities, expertise in budgeting and financial planning, and proficiency in accounting software and systems. The role demands excellent organizational, communication, and interpersonal skills to effectively collaborate with department staff and external stakeholders. A thorough understanding of NCAA regulations, university financial policies, and applicable laws governing financial operations is also crucial.

Creative & New Media

Roles & Responsibilities

The Director of Creative and New Media is pivotal in shaping the digital and creative strategy to enhance the department's brand, engage fans, and showcase student-athletes' achievements across various platforms. This role encompasses oversight of video production, photography, and social media initiatives, often working in tandem with the marketing director or director of external operations. The director leads the development and execution of a comprehensive digital media strategy, including content creation, distribution, and analytics across all digital platforms. They are responsible for managing the athletic department's official website, social media accounts, and other digital platforms to ensure consistent and engaging content that aligns with the department's goals and brand identity. This role involves overseeing the production of high-quality video and photo content, capturing the excitement of athletic events, and telling the stories of student-athletes and teams. They collaborate with coaches, athletes, and department staff to create compelling feature pieces, and promotional videos that enhance fan engagement and support recruitment efforts. Additionally, they analyze the effectiveness of digital content through metrics and feedback, adjusting strategies to optimize reach and engagement.

Requirements

Candidates for this position typically require a bachelor's degree in communications, marketing, digital media, videography, or a related field. A master's degree or specialized training in digital media production, social media management, or graphic design is highly desirable. Key skills include proficiency in digital media software (Adobe Creative Suite, video editing, web development tools), a strong understanding of social media platforms and analytics, and the ability to lead creative projects from conception to completion. The role demands excellent communication and collaboration abilities to work effectively with diverse teams and stakeholders. Creativity, strategic thinking, and a passion for sports and storytelling are also crucial for success in this dynamic and evolving role.

Compliance

Roles & Responsibilities

The primary responsibility of a Compliance Director is to oversee and ensure the athletic department's compliance with NCAA rules and regulations, as well as those of any conferences in which the institution holds membership. This role involves developing and implementing comprehensive compliance policies and procedures that guide coaches, athletes, and staff in maintaining regulatory standards. The Compliance Director conducts regular educational sessions for athletes and staff on NCAA regulations, including eligibility, recruitment, scholarships, and amateurism principles, to prevent infractions. They also monitor and verify the eligibility of student-athletes, manage the recruitment process to ensure it meets all legal and ethical standards, and oversee the preparation and submission of NCAA compliance reports. The role demands meticulous record-keeping and the ability to conduct internal audits to identify and rectify potential compliance issues before they escalate. In cases of alleged violations, the Compliance Director leads investigations and represents the institution in any NCAA proceedings. Their work is crucial in safeguarding the institution's reputation and eligibility for competition.

Requirements

The position typically requires a bachelor's degree in sports management, legal studies, or a related field, with many institutions preferring a master's degree or a law degree due to the complex legal nature of compliance work. Candidates must possess a deep understanding of NCAA regulations, with several years of experience in athletic compliance roles being highly valued. Strong analytical, organizational, and communication skills are essential, as is the ability to navigate complex regulatory documents and effectively communicate these rules to a non-legal audience. Proficiency in compliance software and data management systems is often required. The role demands high ethical standards and the ability to maintain confidentiality when handling sensitive information. Leadership qualities and the ability to work collaboratively with various departments within the institution are also critical for success in this position.

Development

Roles & Responsibilities

The primary responsibility of the Director for Development and Fundraising is to strategize and implement comprehensive fundraising campaigns that support the athletic department's objectives and financial needs. This involves identifying, cultivating, and maintaining relationships with potential donors, including individuals, corporations, and foundations, to garner support for athletic initiatives. The Assistant AD is tasked with organizing fundraising events, such as galas, auctions, and golf tournaments, that engage the community and generate revenue. They also oversee grant writing and sponsorship proposals to secure additional funding sources. Effective communication is crucial, as the Assistant AD often represents the athletic department in public forums and presentations to articulate the value and impact of sports programs on student-athletes' development. They work closely with the marketing and communications teams to promote fundraising campaigns and report on their success to stakeholders. Additionally, the Assistant AD develops stewardship programs to acknowledge and appreciate donors, ensuring long-term support and engagement with the athletic department.

Requirements

Candidates for this position typically require a bachelor's degree in sports management, business administration, marketing, communication, or a related field, with a preference for a master's degree. A minimum of three to five years of experience in development, fundraising, or a similar role within collegiate athletics or a non-profit organization is essential. Strong interpersonal and networking skills are critical for building relationships with donors and community leaders. The role demands excellent organizational and project management abilities to oversee multiple fundraising initiatives simultaneously. Proficiency in donor database software and CRM systems is often required. The Assistant AD for Development and Fundraising must possess exceptional communication skills, both written and oral, for effective donor engagement and public presentations. Leadership qualities and the ability to work collaboratively with various internal departments and external stakeholders are also vital for success in this role.

External Operations

Roles & Responsibilities

The Director of External Operations plays a vital role in managing and enhancing the organization's image, relationships, and revenue opportunities outside its immediate operational sphere. This position focuses on expanding the organization's reach and influence through strategic partnerships, community engagement, marketing initiatives, and media relations. The director is responsible for developing and executing strategies that promote the organization's brand and connect it with fans, sponsors, and the community at large. This includes overseeing marketing campaigns, sports information initiatives, public relations efforts, and social media strategies to increase fan engagement and boost attendance at events. They work closely with the media to ensure favorable coverage of the organization's activities, athletes, and events, managing press releases, media days, and interviews. A significant part of their role involves sponsorship and partnership development. Community engagement is another critical area, with the director organizing outreach programs, charity events, and other initiatives that strengthen the organization's ties to the local community and enhance its public image.

Requirements

This position generally requires a bachelor's degree in marketing, communications, sports management, or a related field, with a master's degree often preferred. Candidates should have at least five years of experience in a similar role, ideally within the sports industry, demonstrating success in marketing, public relations, and partnership development. Strong leadership and communication skills are essential, as is the ability to strategize and execute comprehensive external operations initiatives. Proficiency in digital marketing tools and social media platforms, along with a solid understanding of brand management principles, is necessary. The Director of External Operations must be an excellent negotiator, capable of securing lucrative partnerships and sponsorships. Additionally, they should have a deep understanding of the sports market, current trends, and the ability to adapt strategies to meet evolving challenges and opportunities.

Facility Management

Roles & Responsibilities

The Director of Facility Management coordinates the daily operations of athletic facilities, including scheduling for practices, games, and special events, ensuring optimal use of spaces while minimizing conflicts. They oversee the maintenance and repair of facilities, working closely with maintenance staff to address issues promptly and efficiently. This role involves developing and implementing preventive maintenance programs to prolong the lifespan of facilities and reduce downtime. A significant part of their responsibilities includes ensuring compliance with health, safety, and environmental standards, conducting regular inspections to identify risks, and implementing corrective actions to mitigate hazards. They manage budgets for facility operations and capital projects, overseeing the procurement of equipment and services, and negotiating contracts with vendors and service providers. The director also plays a pivotal role in planning and executing facility upgrades and new construction projects, collaborating with architects, engineers, and contractors to bring vision to reality. They are involved in strategic planning for the athletics department, contributing insights on facility needs and improvements to support the department's goals.

Requirements

Candidates typically require a bachelor's degree in sports management, facility management, business administration, communication, or a related field, with a master's degree preferred. Relevant experience in facility or operations management, preferably in a collegiate athletics environment, is essential, typically three to five years. They must possess strong leadership, organizational, and problem-solving skills, with an ability to multitask and manage complex projects within budget and time constraints. Knowledge of facility maintenance practices, safety regulations, and environmental standards is critical. Excellent communication skills are required for coordinating with internal departments and external contractors, as well as for negotiating contracts. The ability to work flexible hours, including evenings and weekends, is often necessary to support the scheduling needs of athletic events and facility projects.

Game Operations

Roles & Responsibilities

Game operations play a crucial role in ensuring the seamless execution of sporting events and related activities. This position is responsible for the planning, coordination, and management of all logistical aspects of athletic events to provide a safe, enjoyable, and competitive environment for athletes, staff, and spectators. The primary duties of the Game Operations Director involve overseeing the scheduling and execution of all home games, including pre-game preparations, in-game operations, and post-game activities. This includes coordinating with coaching staff, facilities management, security, medical personnel, and external vendors to ensure that all logistical needs are met. They are responsible for compliance with NCAA regulations regarding game operations and ensuring that all events adhere to conference and institutional policies. Key responsibilities also include managing the setup and takedown of venues, overseeing the coordination of travel arrangements for visiting teams, and liaising with broadcast partners to facilitate media coverage. The director works closely with the marketing department to integrate promotional activities into event planning and enhance fan engagement. They are also in charge of emergency planning and crowd control to ensure the safety and security of all event participants and attendees.

Requirements

Candidates for this position typically require a bachelor's degree in sports management, event management, business administration, communication, or a related field. A master's degree in a relevant discipline may be preferred by some institutions. Additionally, a minimum of three to five years of experience in athletic event management or a related area is essential, preferably within an NCAA athletic department. Essential skills include strong organizational and project management abilities, excellent communication and interpersonal skills for coordinating with various stakeholders, and the capability to work under pressure and solve problems efficiently. Familiarity with NCAA regulations and a deep understanding of sports event logistics are crucial. The role demands flexibility, as working evenings, weekends, and holidays is often required to cover athletic events.

Internal Operations

Roles & Responsibilities

The Director of Internal Operations is a pivotal figure, tasked with overseeing the day-to-day administrative and operational functions. This role ensures the smooth functioning of the sports department, aligning operations with the organization's strategic objectives. They oversee the planning, implementation, and evaluation of administrative and operational policies and procedures. This role includes managing the logistics for team travel, coordinating event schedules, overseeing facility management, and ensuring compliance with governing bodies' regulations. The director works closely with coaching staff, athletes, and administrative personnel to ensure that all operational aspects, from equipment management to event execution, are handled effectively. Additionally, this position often entails financial oversight, including budget preparation, monitoring, and reporting to ensure that the department operates within its financial means. They also play a key role in risk management, implementing health and safety protocols to protect athletes and staff. They may be involved in contract negotiations, staff hiring, and training, further ensuring that the department's internal processes contribute to its overall success.

Requirements

Candidates for the Director of Internal Operations position typically need a bachelor's degree in sports management, business administration, communication, or a related field, with a master's degree preferred by many organizations. They should possess at least five years of experience in sports administration or a closely related field, demonstrating a track record of effective operations management. Essential skills include strong leadership and interpersonal abilities to manage diverse teams, excellent organizational skills for handling multiple projects simultaneously, and adeptness in problem-solving and decision-making. Proficiency in office and management software is necessary, as is a thorough understanding of the sports industry's operational standards and compliance regulations. The ability to communicate effectively, both verbally and in writing, with various stakeholders is also crucial for success in this role. The director must be adaptable, able to anticipate and respond to challenges with innovative solutions that support the organization's objectives.

Licensing & Revenue

Roles & Responsibilities

The Director for Licensing and Revenue Generation holds a pivotal position within the athletics department, primarily focused on identifying and capitalizing on revenue opportunities while managing the licensing program for the university's athletic brands and merchandise. This role involves strategizing and implementing initiatives to enhance the department's revenue streams through merchandising, licensing, and various partnerships. The director is responsible for overseeing the licensing process for athletic trademarks and logos, ensuring that all merchandise and products align with the university's brand standards and copyright laws. They negotiate contracts and agreements with vendors, sponsors, and partners, aiming to maximize financial returns while maintaining the integrity of the athletic department's brand. Additionally, they work closely with marketing and communications teams to develop promotional campaigns that drive merchandise sales and engagement with the athletics programs. Analyzing market trends and consumer behavior to identify new licensing opportunities and potential products is a key part of their role. They also collaborate with legal teams to protect intellectual property rights and manage any licensing disputes or infringements.

Requirements

Candidates for this position typically need a bachelor's degree in marketing, communication, business administration, sports management, or a related field, with a master's degree preferred. Experience is critical, with a minimum of three to five years in sports marketing, licensing, or revenue generation within a collegiate athletics department or sports organization. Strong negotiation skills and a deep understanding of copyright and trademark laws are essential. The role demands exceptional strategic planning, financial analysis, and project management abilities. Proficiency in data analysis and market research tools is also necessary. The ability to work collaboratively across departments and with external partners, coupled with excellent communication skills, is crucial for success in this position. The director must be adaptable, innovative, and capable of leading initiatives that drive revenue growth and enhance the visibility of the department.

Marketing

Roles & Responsibilities

The Marketing Director holds a crucial role in promoting the department's sports programs, enhancing fan engagement, and increasing attendance at events. They are tasked with developing and implementing comprehensive marketing strategies that encompass promotions, advertising, digital marketing, and community engagement efforts tailored to the unique needs and goals of the athletic department. This involves creating campaigns that highlight the excitement and competitive spirit of collegiate sports, aiming to boost ticket sales and enhance the game-day experience for fans. They oversee the creation of promotional materials, manage the department's social media presence, and coordinate special events such as pep rallies, fan appreciation days, and community outreach programs. Additionally, the marketing director works closely with sponsors, while ensuring that marketing activities align with the NCAA's regulations. They collaborate with other departments, including ticket sales, media relations, and the teams themselves, to ensure a cohesive and unified marketing effort. They also track the effectiveness of marketing campaigns, analyzing data to inform future marketing strategies and adjust approaches as necessary.

Requirements

Candidates for the position of Marketing Director typically require a bachelor's degree in marketing, sports management, business administration, communication, or a related field, with a master's degree often preferred. Relevant experience of at least five years in sports marketing or a related area is essential, demonstrating a track record of successful marketing campaigns and fan engagement initiatives. Proficiency in digital marketing tools, social media platforms, and data analysis software is necessary. Strong leadership and communication skills are crucial, as is the ability to work collaboratively across departments and with external partners. Knowledge of NCAA regulations and a passion for collegiate sports are also important for success in this role. A marketing director must be creative, adaptable, and capable of managing multiple projects in a fast-paced environment.

Senior Woman Administrator

Roles & Responsibilities

While not a typical role, but instead a title bestowed upon a single female administrator, the Senior Woman Administrator (SWA) is a significant position, advocating for the interests and well-being of female athletes and promoting opportunities for women within the sports programs. The SWA is responsible for overseeing the development and implementation of policies and practices that support gender equity in athletics. This includes monitoring the equitable distribution of scholarships, facilities, equipment, and scheduling to ensure fairness across male and female sports programs. Another key responsibility is serving as a mentor and advocate for female athletes and coaches, providing support and guidance while fostering an inclusive and respectful athletic environment. The SWA also represents the athletic department in NCAA governance, participating in conferences and committees to influence policies affecting women's athletics. Additionally, the SWA is involved in compliance efforts, ensuring that the athletic department meets NCAA and Title IX requirements, and contributes to educational programs and initiatives aimed at promoting understanding and compliance with gender equity principles.

Requirements

Candidates for an SWA position typically require a bachelor's degree in sports management, education, business administration, communication, or a related field, with a master's degree preferred. A minimum of five years of experience in athletic administration, coaching, or a related area within collegiate athletics is essential, demonstrating a commitment to gender equity and an understanding of Title IX regulations. Key skills include strong leadership and interpersonal abilities to effectively advocate for gender equity and navigate complex organizational dynamics. The role demands excellent communication skills, both written and oral, for effective advocacy, policy development, and stakeholder engagement. A thorough understanding of NCAA regulations, particularly those relating to gender equity and compliance, is crucial. The SWA must be adaptable, capable of leading change, and committed to fostering an inclusive and equitable athletic environment.

Sponsorships

Roles & Responsibilities

The Sponsorship Manager plays a crucial role in generating revenue for sports teams, events, and organizations by securing sponsorship deals. This position can be an internal role within a sports organization or contracted out to a third-party property management organization, such as Learfield or Van Wagner, which specialize in managing and selling sponsorships on behalf of their clients. The primary responsibility of the manager is to identify potential sponsors, develop tailored sponsorship packages, and negotiate contracts that meet both the sponsor's and the organization's objectives. This involves researching and understanding the marketing goals of various businesses and how a partnership can provide mutual benefits. The manager is tasked with creating compelling presentations and proposals that showcase the value of sponsoring their sports entity, including brand exposure, engagement opportunities, and hospitality benefits. Additionally, the manager is responsible for maintaining and cultivating relationships with current sponsors, ensuring their satisfaction and engagement with the sponsorship's outcomes. This includes overseeing the fulfillment of sponsorship agreements, coordinating with marketing and event teams to execute sponsorship activations, and evaluating the effectiveness of sponsorship initiatives to provide reports and insights to sponsors and internal stakeholders.

Requirements

This position typically requires a bachelor's degree in marketing, sports management, business administration, communication or a related field. A minimum of three to five years of experience in sales, marketing, or a related area, preferably within the sports, entertainment, or events industry, is essential. The role demands strong negotiation and communication skills to effectively persuade and close deals with potential sponsors. The ability to work independently, manage multiple projects simultaneously, and meet sales targets within tight deadlines is crucial. Leadership skills and the capacity to work collaboratively with cross-functional teams are also vital. For those employed by third-party organizations, a deep understanding of the specific sports properties managed and the ability to align with the organization's overall sales strategies and goals are necessary.

Sports Information

Roles & Responsibilities

A Sports Information Director (SID) plays a crucial role in bridging collegiate athletics with the public, media, and the broader sports community. The SID is tasked with managing all aspects of sports communication and media relations for a college or university's athletic department. Their responsibilities include producing press releases, game notes, and athlete bios, as well as updating the athletics website with schedules, results, and player information. They often handle social media platforms, ensuring timely and engaging content that promotes the department's image and achievements. During sports events, SIDs are responsible for statistic keeping, coordinating media coverage, and ensuring that event information flows smoothly to all stakeholders. They also oversee the production of media guides and game programs, and often serve as the primary liaison between athletes, coaches, and the media, arranging interviews and press conferences. Their role extends to crisis management, where they must handle sensitive issues with tact and professionalism, maintaining the institution's reputation.

Requirements

Typically, a Sports Information Director position requires a bachelor's degree in journalism, communications, sports management, or a related field. This educational background provides the necessary foundation in media relations, writing, and sports marketing. Experience is highly valued, with employers looking for candidates who have previously worked in sports information or media relations, ideally within an athletic department or sports organization. Strong writing skills are paramount, as is proficiency in various social media platforms and sports statistics software. Effective communication and interpersonal skills are crucial, given the collaborative nature of the role and the need to interact with various stakeholders, including media personnel, athletes, and coaches. Additionally, the ability to work flexible hours, including evenings and weekends, is often a requirement due to the scheduling of sports events. Advanced knowledge of NCAA regulations and a commitment to upholding the ethical standards of sports journalism are also important for success in this role.

Ticketing

Roles & Responsibilities

A Ticket Office Director oversees the operations of ticket sales and distribution for sports events, concerts, and other entertainment activities at a venue or for an athletic department. This role is pivotal in ensuring that the ticketing process is efficient, customer-friendly, and maximizes revenue. The primary duty of a Ticket Office Director is to manage the daily operations of the ticket office, including ticket sales, customer service, and financial reporting. They develop strategies for pricing, sales, and distribution of tickets, often utilizing digital platforms to reach broader audiences and improve the ticket-buying experience. They are responsible for ensuring that the ticketing system is secure and user-friendly, implementing the latest technology for online sales, and managing the ticket inventory effectively. This role also involves creating and overseeing the budget for the ticket office, including forecasting revenue from ticket sales. Ticket Office Directors work closely with marketing and promotions teams to develop strategies that maximize ticket sales, such as special promotions, group sales, and early bird pricing. They ensure compliance with legal and ethical standards in ticket sales practices. Additionally, they manage a team of ticket sales agents and customer service representatives, providing training and guidance to deliver exceptional service to ticket buyers.

Requirements

Typically, a Ticket Office Director role requires a bachelor's degree in business administration, marketing, finance, communication, or a related field. This educational background equips them with knowledge in management, marketing strategies, and financial analysis. Several years of experience in ticket sales or a similar field, with a proven track record of successfully managing a ticket office or similar operations, is often required. Strong leadership and team management skills are essential, as is expertise in customer service and conflict resolution. Familiarity with ticketing software and CRM systems is crucial, along with the ability to analyze sales data to inform decision-making. Effective communication skills, both verbal and written, are necessary for this role, as Ticket Office Directors frequently interact with a wide range of stakeholders, from team members to customers and senior management.

Made in the USA
Las Vegas, NV
29 August 2024

94555887R00122